Praise for John Schaub and *Building Wealth One House at a Time*

"For anyone seriously interested in investing in rental houses, John Schaub has been a guru for many years. Not only has he taught thousands of students how to 'make it big on little deals,' but he has brought something to real estate investment that we rarely see in this era of get-rich-quick, flip-this-house-and-make-a-fortune-over-night self-promoters: an unusually strong ethical component that guides his entire approach. In the new second edition of his *Building Wealth One House at a Time*, one of Schaub's core themes is that if you treat people fairly—whether they are prospective tenants looking to rent a house or fellow investors looking to do a joint venture—you will do better. You will prosper in both the long run and the short run. 'When a deal is too one sided,' he writes, 'it will go bad.' There's real financial wisdom in that advice. When deals go bad, you usually don't build wealth. Schaub's book is primarily about the nuts-and-bolts essentials that any small scale investor needs to know."

—Kenneth R. Harney, nationally syndicated
real estate columnist, *The Nation's Housing*

"John Schaub is the 'pope' for real estate investors. Genuine, sincere, no hype, no BS, and his methods and strategies are simple, proven and work in all markets. John is my best mentor ever!"

—Mike Butler, author, *Landlording on AutoPilot*

"John Schaub's steady-Eddie approach to building wealth has worked for his students for over four decades. Here are the rules. 1. Know the local market. 2. Buy a discounted property because you have the knowledge or cash to solve the seller's problem. 3. Rent the property to renters who will stay in the homes for years. In short, buy bargains and offer bargains. Wealth builds, one paid-off mortgage at a time."

—Dr. Gary North, author of sixty-three books, vice president,
Ron Paul Curriculum, editor, *Tea Party Economist* and *Remnant Review*

"Schaub's book is the new gold standard for single-family house investors."

—Jay Decima (Fixer Jay), author of *Investing in Fixer Uppers*

"On my scale of one to ten, it rates an off-the-chart twelve."

—Bob Bruss, nationally syndicated real estate columnist

"John Schaub is the only real estate guru I know who has survived and prospered for forty years in this wild and woolly market."

—Mark Skousen, PhD, presidential fellow,
Chapman University, editor, *Forecasts & Strategies*

"The great thing about this book is that it doesn't promise to make you a real estate millionaire overnight. John Schaub is the real deal! His approach is simple yet effective. Thanks to thirty-five years of experience, John has a consistent and practical approach to buying, financing, and managing houses. If you follow what he teaches, you will enjoy true financial freedom."

—Gary Johnston, author, *Financial Freedom Principles*

BUILDING WEALTH

ONE HOUSE AT A TIME

Updated and Expanded Second Edition

JOHN W. SCHAUB

New York   Chicago   San Francisco   Athens   London

Madrid   Mexico City   Milan   New Delhi

Singapore   Sydney   Toronto

7 8 9   QFR   21 20 19 18

ISBN 978-1-259-64388-0
MHID 1-259-64388-3

e-iSBN 978-1-259-64389-7
e-MHID 1-259-64389-1

Library of Congress Cataloging-in-Publication Data
Schaub, John.
Building wealth one house at a time / John Schaub
Updated and expanded 2nd edition. | New York : McGraw-Hill
   Education, 2016. | Revised edition of the author's Building wealth one
   house at a time, 2005.
LCCN 2016011855 | ISBN 9781259643880 (paperback) | ISBN
   1259643883 | ISBN 9781259643897 (e-ISBN) | ISBN 1259643891 (e-ISBN)
LCSH: Real estate investment. | BISAC: BUSINESS & ECONOMICS / Real
   Estate.
LCC HD1382.5 .S328 2016 | DDC 332.63/24—dc23 LC record available at
   http://lccn.loc.gov/2016011855

McGraw-Hill Education books are available at special quantity discounts to use as premiums and sales promotions or for use in corporate training programs. To contact a representative, please visit the Contact Us pages at www.mhprofessional.com.

This book is dedicated to scrupulous landlords who invest their time and risk their capital to provide decent affordable housing.

And to the dedicated volunteers, staff, and homeowners of the Fuller Center for Housing, who are working together worldwide to eliminate poverty housing.

Contents

Contents

Introduction

Tens of thousands of ordinary people have made millions of dollars investing in the most humble of real estate investments, the single-family house. I am one of them, and I have a unique perspective because I have helped thousands of others make their first million by buying houses.

Buying, renting, and selling houses is not only highly profitable but also helps people in your community. By treating people fairly, you develop a reputation for helping others, and many will refer their friends and family to you when they need to sell, buy, or rent.

By providing a supply of decent, affordable housing, you help young families live near their work while they save enough to buy their own homes. When you buy a house from someone who needs to get rid of it, you relieve him of a burden. When you sell a house and finance it, you often can help someone buy their first home.

Many ordinary people are now millionaires not by winning the lottery but by systematically buying houses. Rather than put their trust in a company pension plan or the government, they have taken control of their financial destiny. By doing what they have done, you can change your life, become financially independent, and be in control of your financial future. It takes less time than you think. Simply follow the advice in this book.

You don't need a lot of education to make a lot of money in real estate. It's not that complicated. In fact, too much education can cause you to overthink and develop analysis-paralysis.

The one thing that keeps most people poor is the fear of buying that first house. Some of my most successful students have taken a year or more to buy their first house. That's fine, as long as you buy it. The second house will be easier, and as you get better at it, you will really enjoy the process of finding and buying a good deal.

MY FIRST HOUSE

It's not even important that your first house is a great deal. The first house I bought, I paid retail price for and made a 20 percent down payment. The good news is that I could rent it for a high enough amount to pay the expenses and pay the loan. The reason it has been one of my best investments is that I still have it. The house is paid for, and it is worth many times what I paid for it.

An investor with a doctorate in finance would never have bought that house, and he would have never held it without refinancing it. He would have been concerned with his rate of return, his lack of leverage, and his running out of depreciation. He would have never turned a $7,000 investment into more than $400,000, not counting the rent that was collected. The annual rent I collect today is more than double my entire down payment.

Building wealth one house at a time does not require a lot of education, money, or even time. It does require one thing—that you buy a house and hold it until it makes you some serious money. This book will show you step by step how you can build your fortune one house at a time.

1

HOW BUYING ONE HOUSE AT A TIME CAN MAKE YOU WEALTHY

Everyone knows something about houses. Ask them, and they will tell you their opinion about what house prices are doing; they even may tell you about a good deal they just missed. Most people agree that a house can be a good investment, yet only a few actually make money investing in houses.

Houses are not complicated, and they're not scary. Their performance is predictable. They produce income when rented, and house rents have a long history of increasing. Likewise, house prices have increased at an average annual rate of roughly 5 percent for about as long as we can measure. They don't go up every year, and in recessions they can drop in price.

When houses are not going up in price, you will make your best buys. The old adage, "You make your money when you buy," has a double meaning when buying houses.

First, you have to buy a house to make money. Just looking won't make you rich. Second, you can make thousands of dollars in profits every time you buy if you buy a house that someone else does not want.

WHY HOUSES ARE YOUR BEST INVESTMENT

After years of investing, I still buy houses instead of apartments or shopping centers. Why? Houses make me more money *with less work* than any other investment.

There is a common conception that apartments or commercial buildings are less work. I've owned both, and I can tell you that this is not true. The tenants in apartments and commercial properties come and go often. Every time they leave, the property will need work. Every time they move, you need to find a new tenant. Tenants in both apartments and commercial buildings are very demanding. They want an immediate response when something breaks. In short, apartments and commercial property are not passive investments. They require hands-on management and an owner who is available 24/7 for problems.

House tenants are different. First, they tend to stay longer. This is a big deal, because a long-term tenant reduces both your maintenance and vacancy expense. My house tenants typically stay five years or longer. That gives me five years of no vacancy and five years of low maintenance expenses. You don't have to repaint the inside or clean or replace the carpet until they leave.

You want to buy property that attracts long-term, low-maintenance tenants—tenants who will pay rent and take care of your property. You want to buy a property that you can rent to tenants who want your house more than you want them.

A side benefit of buying and managing houses is that you can help people sell houses they don't want anymore. You can rent houses to people who need a place to live, and when you sell, you can help people buy their first home. You can solve big problems by buying a house that an owner can't afford and that is ruining their credit. These are all profitable and rewarding experiences.

HOUSES ARE DIFFERENT FROM OTHER INVESTMENTS

Houses are unique investments. You can rent them to provide income, but their value does not depend on that income. Even an empty house can make you money, since it will appreciate as much as a full one. I know investors who buy houses in appreciating areas like San Francisco and never rent them. Many wealthy individuals own many expensive houses in places like Aspen or Palm Beach and never rent them. They are happy with the appreciation alone.

The value of other investment real estate, such as apartments or commercial property, depends on the amount of income it produces. If you rent an apartment or office space for below-market rent, it will be worth less money. An empty house is worth as much as a full one.

Houses Are Safer and More Liquid

Houses are safer investments for several reasons. First, you can buy a house with a smaller investment. You can buy a house with a small down payment, so you have less at risk. Lenders routinely will lend more against a house than any other type of property. And the loans that they make are safer, because they can be for a long term with a fixed interest rate and payment. This makes the payments smaller.

Loans on commercial properties are often shorter in term and some have variable interest rates. A shorter-term loan is riskier, because the payments may be higher and you may have to refinance or sell in a down market.

Next, there are more buyers for houses than for bigger properties. If you need to sell in a hurry, you can—if you offer a house at a good price. Third, houses rent faster and have fewer vacancies. Apartment vacancies often run 10 to 20 percent, whereas house vacancies rarely exceed 5 percent. Commercial properties sit empty for months and even years at a time between tenants. You need a lot of cash in the bank to survive a long-term vacancy in a large building.

WHEN YOU BUY, YOU ARE DEALING WITH AN ANXIOUS SELLER

When you buy a house, typically you are dealing directly with a homeowner who is in a hurry to sell. If the homeowner had plenty of time to sell, then she could wait for a retail price. When you decide to sell any real estate in a hurry, you will have to discount the price to sell it quickly. Learn this lesson: Never put yourself in a position where you have to sell in a hurry.

When you buy commercial or apartment property, you are buying from another investor. You are often dealing with someone who is an experienced negotiator. He might be a better negotiator than you are and that reduces your chances of making a good buy.

When you buy from a homeowner, you have the negotiation advantage. They want to sell more than you want to buy, and you won't buy unless you get the price or terms that you need.

WHEN YOU SELL, YOU WILL GET A RETAIL PRICE AND ALL CASH

More important, when you decide to sell a house, *sell only to a user*. You want to sell to someone who really likes the house, because if they really like your house, they will pay a retail price. I had a potential buyer looking at one of my houses and they called me on their cell phone to ask me a question. I overheard the wife say, "I love this house." I knew then that they would pay full price for the house.

Now, for the really important part! When you sell a house to an owner occupant, that person usually can get a long-term, low-interest-rate loan for nearly the entire purchase price. This allows you as the seller to get a higher price. Plus, when they borrow from the bank to buy your house, you will receive all cash when you sell.

If you want to finance the sale of a house to generate interest income, you have that option. There are always buyers who need help with financing, and often you can sell at an even higher price if you will agree to finance the property for a buyer who cannot qualify for a bank loan. However, if you want the cash to reinvest in another house or just to spend, you can achieve that.

A disadvantage of selling an apartment building or commercial property is that the buyer will be another investor. This investor will not "love" your apartments. They will negotiate to get the best price and terms that they can.

LENDERS PREFER HOUSES

Unlike houses, apartments and commercial properties are not the banks' favorite collateral. Because commercial loans have a higher risk of default and more management responsibility in the event of a foreclosure, banks often limit their commercial loans to 70 percent of value and the term of the loans is often shorter. Often the buyer will not have enough for the down payment, so the deal falls apart, or the seller must agree to finance part or all of the price.

Investment property prices can experience large swings as the economy changes. An empty office building or commercial building will sell for a small fraction of what it cost to build.

A well-located house will appreciate at a greater rate than an average property and will not suffer as dramatic a drop in value as commercial properties during business recessions.

DIVERSIFICATION BRINGS SAFETY AND HIGHER PROFITS

Not all houses perform the same. Higher-priced houses may jump more in price during a boom but can fall in price during a recession. Lower-priced houses are more stable and stay full. It costs a certain amount to buy a lot and build a starter house in your town, and that price is constantly increasing. This supports the lower-priced houses in the market.

A major advantage of investing in several houses rather than one big apartment or office building is that you can diversify by investing in different price ranges. By owning both less expensive and more expensive houses, you can have the safety of the lower-priced houses and the upside potential of the higher-priced ones. Plus, if you needed to raise just a little cash, you could sell just one of your houses. If you owned an apartment building it would be difficult to sell just a part of it to raise cash.

When Average Isn't Average at All

Read reports of prices booming or busting with a little skepticism. Remember that the headline writer's job is to sell newspapers or attract page views, and a spectacular headline is more likely to get him a bonus.

When the press reports that the average price of a house has risen or dropped, that report is often an exaggeration of what is really happening in the market. The average price of a house sold in your town will include the more expensive houses, which are more likely to stop selling when the market cools off.

There is no national house market or national trend for real estate. Although some factors, such as interest rates, the economy, and national security, have national implications, even these affect different housing markets differently. A hurricane in Texas has little effect on the markets in other states.

Housing markets are local in nature. The market in your state can be booming while the next state over is experiencing a recession. In your town, one neighborhood may be appreciating while another is declining in value.

Changes in interest rates will have a more profound effect on house sales in towns where there are a lot of first-time buyers than in a town where many buyers are retired and pay cash for their homes. A threat to national security may drive prices up in areas considered safer while depressing prices in areas perceived as higher risk.

HOW AVERAGES CAN MISLEAD

Suppose that last month four houses sold in your town, and they sold at these prices: $100,000, $150,000, $150,000, and $400,000. The average price of a house sold that month was $200,000. If the following month four other houses sold at $100,000, $150,000, $150,000, and $200,000, the average price of a house sold in your town that month would be $150,000.

Just because the average price of a house sold in your town dropped from $200,000 to $150,000 in one month does not necessarily mean that houses are decreasing in value. It simply means that fewer expensive houses sold that month.

Averages include houses that you don't want to own. Track the prices of houses in neighborhoods that you do want to own. Research what a particular house sold for new and compare it with its resale price to get a real appreciation rate for a neighborhood that interests you.

HOW TO LEARN AND ANTICIPATE
THE REAL TRENDS IN YOUR TOWN

To learn how houses have performed as investments in your town, identify several houses that have sold recently in neighborhoods that you think would be a good place to invest. Research what those houses sold for in previous years. You can find this information in your public records. In the past, this usually meant a trip to the courthouse, but now this information is often available online.

Now calculate how much these houses have increased in value per year on average. Continue to track these houses, and add others to your research as you discover other neighborhoods that you think have potential. This information will help you to identify neighborhoods with a strong history of growth, and you will begin to learn the values in your town.

Neighborhoods and towns are dynamic. They are changing constantly, and you need to become a student of that change. Neighborhoods and towns change like the seasons. If you are paying attention, you can feel, see, and recognize the signs of change early in the cycle. This will enable you to be among the first to buy in a market changing for the better and among the first to sell in a market changing for the worse.

FACTORS THAT AFFECT HOUSE PRICES IN YOUR TOWN

Changes in Population

A growing population will create an increasing demand for housing. If your town is growing in population, then your prices probably will outperform the national average. If your town is losing population, your prices may not increase without inflation and could decline if the loss in population is permanent. People make real estate valuable. Without people, land has little value except to hold the earth together.

Changes in population in nearby communities will also affect your market. If a nearby city is growing rapidly, then it will have a positive effect on your market.

Demographics

When populations change, it's not just in number. As new people move into your town, they will have new needs and demands. If there are young working people moving to your town because of jobs, they will need houses appropriate for children and will want to be near schools and parks that cater to family activities.

If the newcomers are retired, then they may want to be near medical centers, entertainment facilities, and restaurants. The US Census Bureau is a valuable source of information about age, income, family size, and education levels (www.census.gov/housing).

Government Regulation of Developers and Builders

As populations boom and overwhelm roads, parks, schools, and other public facilities, it is typical for the existing population, through the local government, to react and take steps to slow growth. The result is often a steady increase in the cost and time required to develop land and build new houses. Because it costs more to produce a new house, the existing housing market becomes more valuable.

Inflation

Inflation is increasing prices as a result of an increased supply of money and credit. Picture fifty college students in a room. You show up with tickets to a popular sold-out concert that you will sell to the highest bidder, but only for cash. The sales price would be limited to the amount of money in everyone's wallet at the time.

If before you held the auction you gave everyone in the room $100 in cash, then it's pretty predictable that the amount that they would be willing to pay for the tickets would be higher because they had more money. If you would allow them to bid any amount they wanted and would agree to pay you in one year at 6 percent interest, the price bid would be higher still.

The federal government can stimulate economic activity by increasing the amount of money we all have. It does this by both increasing the amount of money in circulation and increasing the amount of money the government lends to banks at relatively low rates. The banks, in turn, can lend this money to consumers and businesses, thereby stimulating buying.

Inflation will drive up the prices of all commodities, including land and house prices. Buying houses protects you against inflation, because both your house prices and rents will keep up with inflation. A leveraged house will allow you to make a dramatic profit with inflation.

Compare prices of commodities that you buy every day with the prices of houses in your town and the rents that they produce. Table 1.1 shows some numbers from my town.

Compare the numbers in your town. The relative value of these items has not changed much. Inflation of the currency has changed the amount of money it takes to buy these items.

Some people are confused by the fact that the prices for some items seem to be cheaper, such as computers. When a new product or technology hits the market, it will be priced high in its early years until the demand increases. This increased demand allows manufacturers to increase production to levels where prices fall because of the economy of producing thousands or millions of the same product. Another factor that can drive down prices is competition. Nothing inspires competition like extraordinary profits.

In inflationary times, you want to invest in assets, such as houses, that protect you from the tremendous loss in purchasing power that inflation causes.

Table 1.1 The Effect of Inflation on Your
Purchasing Power

Year	Commodity	Price
1980	Gasoline	$1.08/gallon
1980	Chicken	$0.55/pound
1980	First-Class Postage Stamp	$0.22
1980	New Chevy Malibu	$6,000
1980	New three-bed, two-bath 1,400-square-foot home	$66,700
1980	Rent for the same house	$425/month
2016	Gasoline	$2.50/gallon
2016	Chicken	$3.00/pound
2016	First-Class Postage	$0.49
2016	New Chevy Malibu	$36,000
2016	New three-bed, two-bath 1,400-square-foot home	$225,000
2016	Rent for the same house	$1,500/month

Inflation hurts the investor with cash in the bank. With $100,000 in 1970 in my town, I could have bought five brand-new homes. With the same $100,000 in 2004, I could buy one-half of a house. If you plan on being here twenty-five years from now, that same house may cost you $2 million.

Inflation also hurts those who invest in fixed-income investments. If you bought an annuity or held a mortgage with payments of $500 a month in 1970, you would have had enough income to buy a new car every four months. With the same income in 2004, it would take you forty months of income to buy the same car.

"Everyone can predict the future. Unfortunately, the future usually pays no attention."

—*Dr. Gary North*

If the next twenty-five years are anything like the last twenty-five, the investor with cash in the bank or holding fixed-income securities or mortgages will be hurt, whereas investors in real estate will benefit.

HOW 5 PERCENT PER YEAR AVERAGE APPRECIATION CAN MAKE YOU RICH

Over the long run, the average house in the United States increases in price about 5 percent per year. How can an investment that goes up 5 percent per year make you rich?

If you buy a house that will produce income, your return will be much higher than 5 percent. If you borrow most of your purchase price, your rate of return could be 30 percent or more.

Suppose that you bought a house worth $200,000 and paid a retail price. If you borrowed 80 percent of your purchase, you would need a 20 percent, or a $40,000, down payment. If the rental income would just cover the monthly payments, and the house appreciated at 5 percent the following year, 5 percent of $200,000 is $10,000, a 25 percent return on your $40,000 investment.

If you learn how to buy a house at below-market prices and then finance even more of the purchase price, your rate of return increases considerably.

Suppose that you bought the same $200,000 house for $180,000 and were able to buy it with a $20,000 down payment. You still get 5 percent appreciation on the full $200,000, so you will earn $10,000 on a $20,000 investment—not accounting for the $20,000 profit you made when you bought the house.

The power in buying real estate on leverage comes in the following years as your profits increase at a compounded rate. The next year your house would be worth $210,000 and go up another 5 percent, or $10,500. The amount the house value goes up increases each year; at the same time, you are paying off debt (see Figure 1.1).

Real estate fortunes are made by buying houses and by then financing them so that you can afford to hold the house until it is free and clear of debt.

Doubling Your Money—The Rule of 72

Do you know how long it takes an investment to double in value if it goes up 5 percent each year? The answer can be calculated by using the mathematical rule of 72, which states that you can calculate the time it will take to double your money by dividing the compounded rate of return (the interest

FIGURE 1.1 Increasing Equity and Decreasing Debt

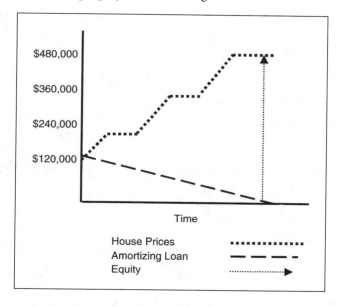

FIGURE 1.2 Number of Years to Double Your Money

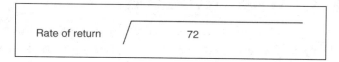

you would earn on a savings account at a bank) into the number 72 (see Figure 1.2).

Thus, 72 divided by 5 equals 14.4. It will take 14.4 years for a house that increases in value at the rate of 5 percent a year to double in value (72/5 = 14.4 years).

DOING BETTER THAN AVERAGE

You want to buy houses that will double your money sooner. You can shorten the time it takes significantly by doing two things:

1. Learn how to buy a house for less than its retail price. The 5 percent average appreciation is based on retail prices. When you learn to buy below retail, your rate of return will be significantly higher.
2. Buy a house in an area with better than average appreciation. Some of my houses have averaged 12 percent a year appreciation. At that rate,

they double about every six years. If I can buy a house at a below-market price that will double in value in six years, I can shorten the amount of time it takes me to turn my 10 percent down payment into $300,000 to four years or less. Look at these results.

Market value	$200,000
Your purchase price	$180,000
Your down payment	$ 18,000
Your loan	$162,000

The house appreciates at 12 percent a year and doubles in value in six years.

Market value in six years:	$400,000
Loan balance in six years:	$150,000
Your equity in six years:	$250,000
Net return on your down payment:	$250,000/$18,000 = enough*

This does not include cash flow produced by the rental income.

BUYING WITH NOTHING DOWN

Read the classic book *Nothing Down*, written by my former student Robert Allen. Robert was a young real estate agent when he took my seminar in the mid-1970s. He bought a number of properties and then wrote about his experience.

You can buy property with nothing down. If you doubt that, look for a property in your town that has been empty for six months or more. Make the owners an offer with nothing down and agree to take responsibility for the property and begin making them monthly payments. When you own an empty property for months and months, the prospect of someone else taking care of it and making monthly payments to you looks good. I know!

Some properties that you can buy with nothing down, you may end up selling for nothing down to the next adventurer. There is a lot of property that

---

*Using the rule of 72, the compounded rate of return can be figured by asking how often $18,000 doubled in six years. The answer is 3.74 (18,000 × 2 = 36,000 × 2 = $72,000 × 2 = 144,000 × 1.74 = 250,000). It doubled then about once every 1.6 years (6/3.7). To calculate the compound annual rate of return, divide 72 by 1.6 and the answer is about 45 percent.

is only attractive to people with no money. As you acquire more money, you acquire better taste in property.

Sometimes great properties are available with nothing down. It's not the property that has the problem; it's the owner. Find an owner who has a big problem that he cannot solve, and you may have found an owner who will sell to you with nothing down.

A local lender foreclosed on a property that was occupied by several tenants and a pit bull. After the dog chased the bank representative off the property, the bank sold the property the next week at way below market and nothing down.

WHEN YOU BUY WITH NOTHING DOWN, YOU OWE IT ALL

When you buy a property with nothing down, you owe the full amount of your purchase price. The terms you get on the money you borrow are more important when you borrow the entire amount than when you buy with less leverage. If you can't make the payments, you will not own the property long enough to make a profit.

You need a plan to generate enough income to repay the loan, or you will soon lose the property. Buying with high leverage is risky business. It is a great way to acquire property when you are starting, but it's like driving a car at a high speed. You need to be totally focused on what you are doing, or there is a good possibility of a wreck.

Another student of mine purchased more than 100 houses—really—the year after he took my class. He bought many of them with nothing down because he was starting out with almost no money.

Unfortunately, he bought faster than he could find good tenants. Eventually, he sold most of these properties for little or no profit because he could not afford to make the payments on a lot of empty houses.

> *If you buy more than you can manage,*
> *nothing down can lead to nothing left.*

Buying 100 Houses—One at a Time

Other investors have accumulated more than 100 houses following my advice to buy them one at a time.

Building Wealth One House at a Time

Buy one, rent one, then—and only then—look for the next deal.

By using this strategy, you will learn management at the same time you learn to buy. Ask yourself this question: If I begin buying houses, will I make a better deal on my first five houses or the last five houses that I buy? If you are learning from the experience, you will make much better buys on the last five houses.

2

BUYING THE HOUSE THAT WILL MAKE YOU THE MOST MONEY

Now that you can see how buying houses can make you money, it's time to get into the specifics of which house you should buy. Having a plan and buying a house that fits into that plan will help you to meet your goals in a shorter time. Most people who buy real estate do not set out to buy a particular property. They just look at everything that is for sale and hope to find a good deal. You can do far better by targeting a house that will make you the most money.

Not all houses are created equal. Some houses will appreciate more; some will produce more cash flow because they will attract better tenants; and others will require more maintenance and have higher expenses. No house is perfect, but you can increase your profits significantly when you target a certain house to buy. Buying houses with a plan will make you more money sooner.

BUYING DIFFERENT HOUSES FOR DIFFERENT REASONS

An advantage of investing in houses is that—over time—you probably will buy more than one. Owning different houses in different neighborhoods allows you to diversify. Some houses will produce more cash flow, and some will appreciate more. Owning houses of different sizes, different ages, and different prices makes your "portfolio" safer than owning one larger property, because your income and expenses are spread over many properties.

When you begin to invest, naturally you will focus on properties that produce more income. Less expensive "starter homes" will produce more cash flow. These homes often are built in tracts where all the lots are the same size and all the houses are about the same size and look a lot alike. They are around 1,000 to 1,200 square feet in total size, with small bedrooms and few frills.

These houses are in high demand and often appreciate at an above-average rate, because few new ones are being produced. Most new houses are larger, more elaborate, and more expensive. The more expensive house typically produces more profit for the builder.

Starter houses rent well and generally rent fast. During hard economic times, tenants often downsize to these houses to save money.

The next step up on the investment ladder is a slightly larger house in a little better neighborhood. There are several reasons to buy these houses as investments.

1. Houses that are a step up from a starter are more likely to attract a longer-term tenant because they have more space and better neighbors. You can buy this size house in a neighborhood that is predominantly owner occupied. Owners take better care of their property than most landlords, so the neighborhood will look better and attract better-looking tenants.

2. If you have other income, pay taxes, and want to reduce your taxable income, you can do that by investing in slightly more expensive houses. A more expensive house can produce larger capital gains but less net rent in relation to its value.

The tax rate on capital gains income is typically significantly lower than the tax rate on ordinary income, such as rental income. If you can buy a more expensive house at a bigger discount, then you are using the tax system to your advantage to earn larger profits and pay less in taxes. Study the example of houses that you can buy in different price ranges shown in Table 2.1.

Table 2.1   Making More, Buying Higher-Priced Houses

Asking Price	Your Purchase Price	Rental Income
$100,000	$90,000	$8,000
$150,000	$135,000	$10,000
$200,000	$175,000	$12,000
$300,000	$260,000	$15,000
$400,000	$350,000	$18,000

These prices and rents represent no particular market, just the principle that as you buy more expensive houses, you are able to buy at bigger dollar discounts. Also, notice that the rents do not increase in direct proportion with the price of the house. The lower-priced houses produce more rental income as a percentage of their value. If the income is important to you, start with the lowest-price house in your town that is in a decent neighborhood.

A high-income taxpayer would have more after-tax profit if he bought a more expensive house, because more of the profit that the house produces would be a capital gain and less would be rent.

BUYING IN THE BEST NEIGHBORHOOD THAT YOU CAN AFFORD

Buyers and tenants are attracted to neighborhoods that are quiet, safe, well maintained, and populated by responsible people. Good neighbors make a good neighborhood. Buy houses in neighborhoods where you feel safe and comfortable talking to the neighbors. The tenant you are likely to rent to probably will look and talk a lot like the people who already live on the street. You need to be able to relate well to your tenant, so you should relate well to the neighbors.

Good neighbors are attracted by many factors, including geography. High ground, the right exposure, and proximity to roads, rivers, lakes or oceans, hospitals, work, and schools are all factors that affect desirability—and therefore value. Study the geography in your town and learn why certain areas are more popular and therefore more valuable.

Schools have a significant effect on neighborhood values. Get to know which schools in your areas are the most desirable. Become knowledgeable about which schools are improving and which are becoming less desirable. Watch for information about planned new schools and possible redistricting. Both tenants and buyers will want to live in the best school districts that they can afford. Often new schools are popular and attract both good teachers and good students.

Buy in the best neighborhood that you can afford. A house in a better neighborhood will make you more money. If you are beginning with little, then still buy in the best neighborhood that you can afford. As you build more cash and cash flow, you will be able to afford to move up a notch in location.

BUYING A HOUSE THAT WILL ATTRACT A LONG-TERM TENANT

When you buy a house that you want to hold as an investment, you want it to be attractive to good tenants—tenants who will stay a long time and take good care of your property. You want to rent to a tenant with long-term potential, not someone who is constantly on the move. Tenants with the long-term potential typically are coming out of another house where they have accumulated furniture and lots of other stuff. You want to buy a house that has enough space for such a tenant to live in comfortably.

The overwhelming majority of homebuyers prefer at least a three-bedroom, two-bath house. Renters have the same preferences. If you buy a smaller house, you will have to compete at a disadvantage with all the three-bedroom houses in your town for rent. There is not a big difference in price between a two-bedroom and a three-bedroom house, but there is a big difference in demand. The three-bedroom house will rent faster and stay rented longer. Buy houses that have three or more bedrooms.

Larger houses containing four or five bedrooms are common in communities with larger families. They also appeal to extended families where several generations share a house. This trend will increase as house prices and rents continue to rise. These larger dwellings have higher maintenance, but they can be as profitable when there is demand for them as rentals. You would learn about this from your research before you start making offers.

Garages or basements are big pluses both when you sell and when you rent. Storage space is important to everyone. Again, the cost of buying a house with a garage or basement is not that much higher, but the garage or basement is a big advantage when you rent or sell.

Yards are a big selling point to families with children and pets. In my town, most tenants have both, so having a fenced back yard makes it easier to rent or sell. Tenants will maintain a yard but rarely will improve one. Look for houses with average-size yards for your town. A large yard may scare off tenants who see it as too big of a job. The lack of a back yard that kids can play in is a definite disadvantage. A nearby park can compensate for a small yard.

SOME HOUSES ARE TOO BIG OR TOO FANCY FOR INVESTMENT

While you can argue that once you own the lot and the house, a few extra square feet costs little money to add, in reality, every square foot you add to a house does cost you. The fixed costs such as taxes and insurance increase with size and value, and so does the cost to maintain the house.

An investment house should be big enough to attract an average-size family with their belongings, but not much bigger. I would be comfortable living in any of my rental houses, because the neighborhoods are quiet and the neighbors are friendly. However, the investment houses are smaller and lack some of the luxury items that you may be used to in your own home.

Buy a house that is functional and well located, and then keep it in good operating condition. Don't buy a house with a lot of fragile items such as fancy wallpaper, trim, elaborate landscaping, and so on. The tenants won't take care of it, and it will not look as good in a year as it does today. Avoid houses with high-maintenance frills such as pools and hot tubs. They are expensive to maintain and insure, and only a small percentage of the buying and renting population will pay the price to have such things.

IT'S THE LOT THAT GOES UP— NOT THE HOUSE

Every day a house is wearing out and becoming obsolete. It's the lot that is becoming more valuable. To make the most money, you want to buy the best lot that you can, and hopefully that lot will be improved with a house that you can rent to a decent tenant while you wait for the lot to make you some serious money.

Some lots are better than others. Avoid lots on busy streets or strangely shaped lots. Even corner lots are not as valuable as interior lots. With a corner lot, you have to set the house back from two streets. This leaves you with a big front yard on two sides but an unusually small back yard. Although corner lots are good for model homes, most owners would rather have a back yard. Always walk the lot line and look over any fences. If there is a problem property or neighbor next door, learn about it before you buy. You can fix a house, but it's a lot harder to fix a bad neighbor.

The location of the lot is the key to how much money you will make in the long run. The advantage of buying several houses for investments is that you can target three or four neighborhoods in your town that you feel will appreciate at better than average rates. If you buy in all three or four, then you are likely to hit a couple of hot areas that will give you a larger than average profit.

BUY IN A NEIGHBORHOOD
THAT IS ON THE WAY UP

Neighborhoods are changing constantly. When they are new, most neighborhoods are almost totally owner occupied. As the houses age, some owners will rent their houses or sell to investors who will rent them. The rental houses are rarely maintained as well as owner-occupied houses, and they have a negative effect on values. Sometimes the neighborhood will become completely owned by landlords. You can spot these streets by a lack of pride of ownership.

If these neighborhoods are in good locations, eventually owners will begin moving back in and buying bargains that they can fix up and live in. When this happens, property values will start to appreciate rapidly. Study the neighborhoods that interest you to see if you can establish where they are in this cycle. Buy in an area that is improving, and you will make more money.

FINANCING DETERMINES
YOUR CASH FLOW

Your ability to borrow and to make down payments will change with time. You may start with little money and no credit. You can still buy a house. You

will need to find a nontraditional source of financing, such as owners who will sell you their house and finance the purchase for you.

I have never borrowed money from a bank to buy a property.

When I started investing in real estate, I was working as a commissioned real estate salesman with no history of producing income and no predictable income. The banks would not make me loans to buy property because I had no demonstrable way to pay the loans back.

As I began to buy houses and accumulate both equity and cash flow, the bankers began courting my business. By then I had found both faster and cheaper sources of money. To this day, I have never borrowed money from a bank to buy a house.

Other investors, sellers of property, and private lenders provide a source of both down payments and long-term financing. In Chapters 8 and 9 you will learn to use all three.

The terms of your financing will determine if you can buy a house with the down payment that you have and afford the payment each month. Ideally, you will be able to borrow on a long-term, fixed-rate loan. With a fixed-rate loan, you get to keep the profits as your rents increase. With a variable-rate loan, the lender will make more money as interest rates rise.

A long-term loan is important to you if you plan on holding a house for investment. The longer-term loan will have lower payments. Low payments make this a safer investment. Avoid short-term loans. You may have to sell or refinance to pay them off. If interest rates are higher when you have to sell or refinance, you may end up paying a much higher interest rate or selling at a discount.

As the economy changes, you will borrow at different interest rates. When rates are the highest, you will make your best buys. When rates drop, you will be able to borrow at low rates and refinance your high-interest-rate debt, increasing your cash flow.

PRODUCING CASH FLOW

The cash flow a house produces depends on both its financing and its ability to produce income. If you finance the house with a long-term, low-interest-rate loan, then you have won half the battle.

The other half of the challenge is buying a house that will attract long-term tenants and will have average or below-average operating expenses, such as taxes, insurance, and maintenance.

Before you buy, research the property taxes and learn if they will change if you buy the house. Property taxes often increase when a property is sold. Contact a local insurance agent and get an estimate of what it will cost to insure a house of the construction and age you are considering.

Estimating the maintenance cost is more difficult. A well-designed, well-built, and well-maintained house should be cheaper to maintain. A house that has an older roof and mechanical systems will cost more to operate. An experienced home inspector or friendly building contractor can look over a house and give you advice about how much maintenance that house is likely to require. Don't ask someone whom you might hire to do repair or maintenance work to inspect the house. That's like asking your barber if you need a haircut.

RENTING TO RESPONSIBLE TENANTS

We all have little personality quirks. It bothers me when people don't take care of things. If I loan you something, I'd like you to return it—and return it in good condition.

This can be a problem when you loan someone a nice house to live in, and then they don't take care of it. Yes, they pay rent to live there, but that does not give them the right to abuse your property.

The good news is that if you buy a decent house on a safe street, you can attract tenants who will take good care of it. I have had hundreds of tenants—and only a few bad ones. One measure of your success as a landlord is the number of tenants you have to evict, that is, legally force to leave your house. I have had to evict only six tenants. The others have paid as agreed and taken reasonable care of the property.

This record with tenants is not just good luck. I learned many of my lessons the hard way—by making expensive mistakes. Hopefully, you won't have to repeat the same mistakes to learn the lesson.

One of my first investments was a brand-new nine-unit apartment building. It was a beautiful property, and I thought that I would own it forever—until I met the tenants. I thought that there would be a certain efficiency in having nine tenants living close together. Collecting the rent should be easy: just drop by on the first of the month and pick up my money.

The first month I dropped by to find only one tenant home. There were plenty of cars in the parking lot, but after I knocked on the first door, no one else would answer. It took me nine visits to sneak up on all nine tenants, and after all of that effort, I still got several stories and promises to pay rather than actual rent.

Here I was, a young, poor landlord who needed every rent check from that building to make the mortgage payment. The tenants saw me as a wealthy landlord, but the truth was that they drove better cars than I did. To add insult to injury, many had bigger TVs than I did too, yet they would not pay me the rent.

It was a cultural difference. These tenants came from a culture where if you could talk the landlord out of the rent, it was a good thing. I learned that I wanted to own property that would attract tenants who felt that paying the rent on time was a good thing and would feel some remorse if they were late.

A TENANT—NOT TOO RICH AND NOT TOO POOR

Your first reaction might be that a tenant can't be too rich. The problem with a rich tenant is that she won't stay long. She will buy, and you will have a vacancy again.

Tenants certainly can be too poor. People are poor because they don't have any money. There may be a lot of good reasons why they don't have any money, but if they don't have money, they will not pay the rent.

I divide potential tenants into three broad groups. Those with too much money, those without enough money, and those with just the right amount of money. Obviously, I want to buy a house that the last group can afford and wants to rent.

The amount of money that good tenants earn varies from place to place. Most of my tenants have hourly or commission jobs and earn between two and three times the base wage in my town. Often there is more than one wage earner in the family. Their income should be close to three times the rent. If they have several children and a car payment, they will need more. Many tenants have enough income to afford to buy a house if they would just pay off their bills and save up a down payment. Those two obstacles are insurmountable for most.

Study your market. Don't rent to people at either end of the income range in your town. Aim at tenants who make enough money to afford your rent and their other normal expenses. Later you will learn about tenant screening and selection.

BUYING YOUR FIRST HOUSE

You want your first house investment to be a success, especially if you are married. You increase your chances of success by buying close to where you live. It may not be in your neighborhood, but it should be as close as possible. Most people live only a few minutes from an area of houses that would make good investments.

When you target an area close to where you live, you can spend time in that neighborhood and really learn the market. Walk the streets and talk to the neighbors. Tell them that you want to buy a house in their neighborhood and ask them if they know of anyone who wants to sell. You are complimenting them on living in a nice neighborhood. You will be surprised at how helpful they will be.

Call on every house for sale and for rent until you know the market well enough that you can walk down a street and give a price and rent for each house. Use a range: it would sell for between $200,000 and $225,000, or it would rent for between $1,400 and $1,500. You are making the assumption that the houses are in rentable condition and, of course, would offer less on a house that needed work. When a house comes on the market, you will know what it is worth and what it will rent for. You can confidently make an offer, knowing that if the owner accepts, you have made a good deal.

3

REAL ESTATE BUBBLES, CRASHES, AND CYCLES

WHAT CAUSES A REAL ESTATE BUBBLE?

A housing bubble is caused by the speculation of many homebuyers and homebuilders. Speculation is buying with the hopes of a large profit, and at the same time taking a large risk.

The large risk in real estate speculation is made possible by lenders that allow homebuyers and builders to borrow a high percentage of the purchase price, even when they have no way to repay, except from increasing house and land prices.

During the last housing bubble that peaked in 2007, many buyers surpassed a nothing-down purchase by borrowing more than they paid for the property. A speculator would buy a house for $250,000, obtain a $225,000 first mortgage and a $75,000 second mortgage. Their plan was to use the proceeds from the second mortgage to make the payments on the first until they sold the house at a profit.

Of course, when real estate prices peaked and reversed, most of those who had speculated gave the property back to the lender, causing a huge amount of foreclosures. The foreclosed properties then sold at bargain prices, for far less than it would cost to produce them, and dragged the prices of the nonforeclosed prices down with them. This caused many nonspeculators to lose their homes as prices dropped 50 percent or more as markets crashed.

Millions of homes were then bought at bargain prices by investors and hedge funds set up to take advantage of properties selling for far less than their worth. These properties could be rented for immediate returns that exceeded "normal" rental returns.

The federal government can contribute to bubbles by creating programs that allow homebuyers to buy with little or nothing down and with reduced requirements for income and credit. The foreclosure rate when someone has little or nothing invested and marginal income and credit is often high.

A downturn in housing markets can be caused by many things, including a problem in a local economy, like a major military base or employer closing. It could be caused by the national economy tanking or, like in 1986, a major revision in the federal tax code.

You might foresee some of these events, but probably you won't. If smart people could foresee major changes in the economy, why would the biggest and smartest investors in the world get caught holding billions in bad mortgages?

CRASHES CAN BE REGIONAL

A crash in another state may not affect your market at all. Often crashes occur regionally when builders overbuild and lenders overlend. This creates too many houses and prices will flatten or fall.

If a crash is a result of rampant speculation, but you live in a conservative part of the country where buyers do not borrow as much, then your market may not be as affected. Many conservative markets just chug along with small increases in prices and rents each year.

Other markets, like Florida, seem to have recurring booms and busts. If your prices are rising at 15 or 20 percent a year, you should suspect that a change is coming.

Study the history of prices and rents in your town. If you live in an area of low but steady growth, your cycles may be mild. If you live in a booming area, know that booms are often followed by busts, and plan for them.

Six Signs Your Market Might Be Near the Top

1. It's too easy to borrow money. Lenders are soliciting you.
2. Everyone is buying, all of your friends, your tenants, your yardman, your yardman's kids.
3. Prices are moving up much faster than rents.
4. Buyers are overleveraging property.
   - The seller has bought a new house, and it closes in two weeks.
   - Their payments cannot be made with the rent the property produces.
   - Buyers are able to buy with "nothing down."
5. Builders are speculating in both land and houses. They are building with borrowed money hoping to find a buyer at a profit. They also borrow to buy land for future building.
6. Without appreciation, there would be no profit. With an investment, you make a reasonable return from the net rents that you collect, without appreciation. Appreciation is a bonus, not your primary source of profit.

HOW A CRASH CAN BE GOOD FOR YOU

A crash in your market may actually be good for you, if you are ready for it. A real estate crash drives the prices of property below their actual value. A house that costs $150,000 to build, and rents for $1,400 a month, might be bought for $100,000 after a crash.

In my market in Florida and in many other towns, houses appreciated from $125,000 to $250,000, then crashed back to less than $150,000—all in a five-year period. Investors were then able to buy a house worth $150,000 for $100,000 because no one else was buying.

GETTING READY FOR THE NEXT CRASH

A successful long-term investor is prepared to prosper in any market. Here are ways you can prepare:

1. Know your market prices and rents.

In a rapidly changing market, it's challenging to keep up with changes in prices and rents. An active landlord who is constantly buying and renting property has the best information. Lenders and appraisers will be dealing with outdated information. What happened last year or last month is not an accurate indicator of today's market.

This time lag between actual values and last month's values gives the active investor an advantage over those who rely on historical statistics. Because appraisers are always relying on yesterday's sales, their appraisals will be high or low depending on the direction of the market.

2. Have some cash in the bank, or know where and how to get it.

A successful investor has the benefit of large cash flows and the luxury of keeping enough cash on hand to take advantage of downturns in the market. However, a new investor is likely to be fully invested, with little cash on hand. An investor is more at risk in his or her early years because he or she has little in cash reserves.

There are alternatives to having cash in the bank. One is a line of credit that you could draw on if you needed it to survive, or to buy a bargain. A line of credit might be secured by your home. If you do that, know that you are risking your home to buy an investment.

An unsecured line of credit can be available from a bank or credit union. These typically need to be repaid within a short time, and most require monthly payments.

A second source is an investor with cash that would fund your purchase if you found a great deal but were short on cash. More on this in Chapter 9.

A third source of cash would be equity in a property that you could borrow against (or sell) to get some cash to buy bargains.

And the fourth source of cash is the knowledge of how to buy without banks. You will learn more about this in Chapter 8.

3. Rent to tenants with diversified employment.

If all of your tenants are in the building business, they may all leave when the building stops. Tenants with multiple sources of income are more likely to survive a bad recession.

4. Embrace change.

Successful long-term investors *embrace* change. They anticipate it, look forward to it, and don't panic when it occurs. As mentioned in my book *Building Wealth in a Changing Market* (McGraw-Hill, 2007), "Successful investors not only adapt to change, they exploit it. While the majority sit on the sidelines wringing their hands, successful investors are looking for and buying opportunities created by the change."

While it's impossible to predict the future or when your market will change, the first person who recognizes the change will be the one who has the best chance of surviving and profiting.

STRATEGIES FOR SURVIVING MARKET CRASHES

1. *Own something free and clear.* You may not own a house free and clear when you are starting, but you might own your car, your tools, or maybe a part interest in a property. A great goal is to get your home paid for.

2. *Use options to buy in a hot market.* An option to purchase real estate is a contract that gives the buyer the right, but not the obligation, to buy. If prices drop, then the buyer can choose not to close.

3. *Avoid personal liability on dangerous debt.* Dangerous debt is described in Chapter 7 as debt that you cannot repay from the cash flow on the property that is security. If you lose this property in foreclosure, then your other assets could be at risk.

4. *Limit your losses.* If you own a losing property, the faster you sell it, the less you will lose. A property that costs you a lot to own each month and that is declining in value can consume all of your money and a lot of your time. Dump it fast, and you might have a chance to make your money back by buying a bargain.

5. *Renegotiate debt that you cannot pay.* A lender that is not getting paid in a declining market does not want to repossess property. They too want to limit their losses and will renegotiate the terms of debt that you owe them to avoid a foreclosure or possible bankruptcy. Ask them to forgive late fees, reduce your payments, and even reduce your principal balance.

THE CAUSE AND EFFECT OF CYCLES

Rent and Price Cycles

House prices and rents do not typically rise or fall in tandem. When rents are cheap, renters are happy to stay renters. When house prices start rising, more people become interested in buying. More buyers can mean fewer tenants, and result in stable or even dropping rents.

Be aware of the relationship between rents and prices in your town. When rents are cheap relative to prices, then either the rents will increase or the selling prices will fall. Conversely, when rents are high compared to selling prices, more will want to buy and selling prices are likely to rise.

CREDIT CYCLES

When loans for acquiring houses are easily available, prices move up sharply as more buyers compete for a limited supply of houses.

After a recession, bankers are slow to reenter the market. They want to make sure of the trend before lending. Recessions are often followed by legislation designed to prevent the next recession. These new laws also slow a recovery.

CONSTRUCTION CYCLES

When builders can build and sell at a profit, more will enter the market until the market becomes overbuilt. National builders are self-financed through the sale of their companies' stock, so they are not as limited by the availability of credit.

Smaller homebuilders rely on banks for construction loans. These loans are typically one year in length. When they can't sell, they are under pressure from the bank to liquidate and pay off the loan. You can buy houses at a bargain price in a down market by just paying off the construction loan.

NEIGHBORHOOD CYCLES

Neighborhood cycles are as important as broad economic cycles. A brand-new neighborhood may look inviting, but it might not look this good again for thirty years.

New houses are often bought by buyers at premium prices and with large loans. The next recession could cause many foreclosures as highly leveraged homeowners walk away from their mortgages. The result is that these homes are often bought by investors who will rent them.

When renters displace owner occupants in a neighborhood, the quality of the neighborhood and the price of the houses declines.

Older neighborhoods where renters are being displaced by owner occupants who buy and fix up a well-located but older home will increase in value. Look for this trend and houses that you can rent for a few years while the neighborhood improves. They often are a better investment than new neighborhoods.

These older neighborhoods often have many free-and-clear houses so there will be fewer foreclosures and short sales during a crash. This gives these neighborhoods more price stability.

HOUSE CYCLES

Houses, too, have cycles: from new, to dated, but still functional, to too old to fix. Most houses I buy are in the middle category and can be kept functional for decades with routine maintenance. Although you can fix any house, it is not economically feasible to bring back most old houses. At some point it makes more sense to tear them down and build new.

Changing Your Strategy as Markets Change

As markets change, you can buy more property when prices are favorable, and sell your weaker properties when prices are higher and it's easy to sell.

It's a mistake to try to sell all of your properties at what you think is the top of the market, and then to try to buy back in at the bottom. If you have acquired easy-to-manage houses in neighborhoods with potential, financed so that you have cash flow, don't sell them just because they go up in price. These are the investments that will produce profit for you every day that you own them. In addition, good tenants are assets. If you sell and then buy back in a few years, you will have to do a lot of work to replace them.

What Part of the Cycle Is Your Market Today?

You can't know the future, but you can be aware of your market direction today. Are your prices rising or falling? Is it easy or hard to find good tenants? Can you borrow on terms that allow you to make a profit?

When it's easy to borrow, it's typically easy to sell and harder to rent. When it's hard to borrow, you get your best buys and often the rental market is stronger.

There Is Always Opportunity, Whatever Your Market Is Doing

You can find a great buy in any market if you look hard enough and look in the right places. I prove this when I teach my class on acquiring and managing houses once a year in my hometown. In the class students go into neighborhoods and find a great opportunity, often in just a couple of hours. Some years they find a dozen opportunities in a short time. Other years they have to work harder to find an opportunity, but they keep looking until they do. If you're interested in learning more about my classes, you can see my class schedule at www.johnschaub.com.

There are a lot of houses, most owned by owner occupants and a lot of them sell every year. According to the US Census Bureau, there are more than 82 million detached, owner-occupied, single-family houses in the United States (www.census.gov/hhes/www/housing).

There are approximately 115 million total occupied (owned and rented) housing units in the United States and more than 60 percent of houses are owner occupied. Just under 5 million (4,940,000) existing homes were sold according to data from the National Association of Realtors®. Another 437,000 newly constructed homes were sold in 2014, according to the US Census Bureau. Over the long term, houses have a history of appreciating prices (see Figure 3.1).

FIGURE 3.1 Median Prices of Houses Sold in the United States, 1975–2015

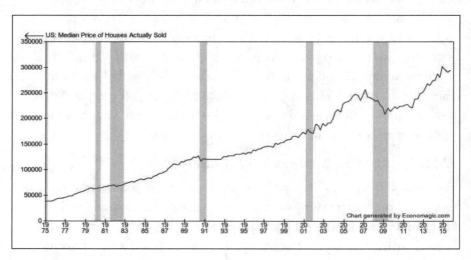

4

FINDING OPPORTUNITIES THAT OTHERS MISS

Now that you know the price range and size of the house you want to buy, you can begin looking for opportunities. This can be overwhelming because there are often many properties for sale. Focusing on certain neighborhoods and specific types of properties in those neighborhoods will help you to identify the houses you want to research and then to make an offer.

SOURCES OF OPPORTUNITIES

A great thing about buying houses for investments is that there is an unlimited supply of opportunity. Every day new houses come on the market. Every day people's lives change unexpectedly, and they decide to sell their house. Every day brings new opportunities.

One of my teachers, Warren Harding, encouraged me to look for good deals close to where I lived and worked. He advised me to never drive down the same street twice. Instead, drive down different streets in different neighborhoods and you will constantly see new opportunities. Real estate opportunities are everywhere, yet some investors drive for hours or even go to other states trying to find greener grass. They drive past or fly over thousands of opportunities near where they live.

Out-of-town management can be an expensive adventure. I know first-hand: I've owned investment properties in ten states. Today I only own property in the town where I live. Owning property close to you allows you to stay on top of the management or to manage it yourself. Even more important, you know your market and can buy when there are buying opportunities and sell when the market is hot.

Most buyers look at properties listed for sale. *The best opportunities are not on the market for sale. They are not listed, and there is no sign in the front yard.*

When you can identify a house that an owner wants to sell and that is not listed, you have no competition from other buyers. Here are my top sources of opportunities for investment homes:

1. *Empty houses.* Not all empty houses are opportunities, but most opportunities are empty houses. An empty house is costing somebody money every day. In addition, it is a source of worry and work for someone. Look for empty houses, and contact the owners. If the house is empty, knock on the neighbor's door and ask if he knows where the owner has moved. If that fails, look up the neighbor's phone number and call him. Neighbors typically don't like an empty house next door, especially if it is not being maintained. Neighbors can be a valuable source of information. The owner may be a lender who has foreclosed or an heir who has inherited the property.

2. *Houses that need work—especially in nicer neighborhoods.* Houses in disrepair stand out, especially on a good street. Some people are just poor housekeepers, but more often they are short of money to repair the house. Occasionally, the house is rented to a tenant who is not maintaining it. All these situations signal potential profit.

3. *Out-of-town owners.* While you cannot see this from the street, you often can find an owner's name and address in the public records. When you spot an empty house or one in disrepair, look up the owner. This can often be done on the Internet. If not, go to your county courthouse and ask for help in looking up a property's owner. While you are there, ask how to find out if there are any mortgages or liens against the property,

and read those. You can learn what the current owner paid and what he or she owes.

4. *Landlords who are not maintaining their property.* When you see an occupied house in disrepair, knock on the door and ask if it is for sale. If it is rented, the tenant typically will tell you and may even give you the landlord's name and phone number. If the landlord is out of town, he may be more than willing to sell. You can tell the tenants that if you buy it, you would be willing to fix it up and maybe rent to them. Sometimes the tenant is the problem, and sometimes the problem is the owner.

Some houses are occupied but not rented. Either the tenants have quit paying rent and the landlord has done nothing to correct the problem, or sometimes a relative or friend has moved int-o a house to "house sit" or take care of it until it sells.

If the tenant or "house sitter" is not a good house and yard keeper, it detracts from the house and makes it harder to sell.

5. *For sale by owners (FISBOs).* Many owners try to sell their property without the help of a broker. Some of these owners do not have enough equity to pay a broker, and you can buy their house simply by taking over their payments. Other sellers may own their property free and clear and be willing to finance the purchase. Still others have had bad experiences with brokers and may be anxious to get rid of a house that is a problem to them. Their problem may be your opportunity. Before you go to see their house, research what they paid for it and what they might owe in the public records. Ask them the questions listed on pages 37 through 39. Don't waste your time and energy going to see a house until you are sure that it is an opportunity that you want to buy.

6. *Real estate agents.* Although some of my best buys have been from agents, they are a *seasonal* source of deals. When the market is hot, they don't need buyers, so you won't get many calls. When the market cools off, they have more sellers than buyers, and they will call you. Ask a lot of questions when they call to qualify the house. They will try to sell you anything they have listed. Don't waste your time unless you smell opportunity.

7. **Lenders.** Like agents, lenders are a seasonal source of good buys. When the economy softens and lenders foreclose on many loans, they need buyers and will be cooperative in selling you properties at wholesale prices. When the market is hot, they have few foreclosures and don't need buyers.

8. **Letters to owners who may need to sell.** Sending out letters and post-cards to sellers who may have a financial problem can be very productive. However, this process costs money and requires a good system so that you follow up on leads aggressively. I have walked into a house of a seller in foreclosure and seen a pile of letters from buyers who have written trying to buy the house. I bought the house because I knocked on the owner's door and talked with her. If you could send out 1,000 letters at a cost of $1 each and get one good lead and buy one good deal, would the letter be a good investment? Of course, but it takes effort to write a good letter and send it to the owners in trouble to the right addresses. **You don't buy houses with letters, you generate leads.**

9. **Foreclosures.** Many good buys are made because the seller has a financial problem, so a house in foreclosure seems like an obvious opportunity for an investor. However, only a few houses in foreclosure are in the price range and neighborhoods where you want to buy. A high percentage of foreclosures have loans far greater than their value. Look for foreclosure opportunities in the neighborhoods where you want to buy and follow up by knocking on the door. The best deals will not have a sign in the front yard or an ad in the newspaper. The way you will find them is to walk through neighborhoods and knock on doors.

ASKING QUESTIONS TO KNOW WHAT THE OTHER PARTY WANTS

If you are calling on an ad in the paper or someone has called you, before you hop in your car to go see the house, ask the person a few questions. The answers to these questions will help you to decide which houses are potential deals and which sellers you want to meet.

If you are walking through a neighborhood and find a house that looks like an opportunity, you want to ask the owner these same questions.

Finding Opportunities That Others Miss

In a normal market, 90 percent of the houses for sale are not opportunities. You are trying to identify that one seller in ten who might have a reason to make you a good deal. After you find the right seller, you want to determine whether this house has the potential of making you money. Not all houses are opportunities.

Asking the right questions gives you clues about how anxious the seller is to sell the house, and then the information will help you to make an offer that the seller can accept. It will increase your chance of buying a house at a good price.

Ask these questions to determine a seller's motivation to make you a good deal. The first questions will be easy for the seller to answer. As you ask the harder questions, you are both gathering information and testing the seller's eagerness to sell. If the seller keeps answering questions, eventually the information you receive is not really in the seller's best interest to share with a potential buyer. Keep in mind that the seller is answering the questions to keep you interested in the house because he or she really wants to sell it.

As you ask these normal questions, take notes, because you will learn a lot. Number a sheet of paper (or take notes on your computer) and record the answers to the following questions:

1. *Are you the owner?*
   Many times a neighbor or relative will answer the phone for an out-of-town owner. If so, ask for the owner's cell phone number and call him or her directly.
2. *Where is the house?*
   Only pursue houses in neighborhoods where you want to own property. Write down the address and phone number.
3. *How large is the house?*
   Look for houses large enough to accommodate a family.
4. *How old is the house?*
   Older houses may be in great neighborhoods, but beware of fragile and high-maintenance houses.
5. *How large is the lot?*
   Look for lots of normal size and regular shape with adequate front and back yards.
6. *Does the house need any work?*
   All houses need some work. Look for an honest answer.

7. *What school districts is the house in?*
   Know which schools are the best and worst in your town. Buy in the best districts that you can afford.
8. *What are the neighbors like?*
   Are there more tenants or owners on the street?
9. *How long have you owned the house?*
   Long-term owners often have larger profits and are easier to negotiate with.
10. *Have you made any additions or remodeled?*
    Not all additions or remodeling projects add value to a house, but new plumbing, electrical service, roofs, kitchens, and bathrooms are big pluses.
11. *Is the house listed with a Realtor?*
    If so, when does the listing expire?
12. *Do you have a current appraisal?*
    If yes, ask how much it appraised for.

These are warm-up questions. They let the seller know that you are interested and give you some basic information. If at this point you are interested in the house, move on to the following, more probing questions.

The questions that follow are ones that you should give the owner plenty of time to answer:

1. *It sounds like a great house, so why are you selling?*
   Listen!
2. *Can your existing loan be assumed?*
   The owner may not know, but most loans can be assumed with the lender's permission.
3. *What is the balance on your loan now?*
   This will tell you how much equity the owner has.
4. *Are your payments current?*
   Surprising enough, most owners will tell you.
5. *What will you do if you don't sell?*
   Is the owner moving anyway? When? The day before they move, most owners are really ready to make a deal.
6. *How long has your house been on the market?*
   This time! Most people answer two weeks, but it's the third time they have tried to sell.

7. *How much did you pay for the house?*

If the owner balks at this question, tell him or her that you want to buy in a neighborhood that is appreciating. Ask if the house has appreciated since he or she bought it. In addition, you can point out that you can learn this information in the public records and would appreciate his or her time-saving assistance.

8. *If you don't sell the house, would you consider renting it?*

If the owner answers yes to this question, you may be able to buy it from him or her with a small down payment. The owner won't get much down when he or she rents it.

With hundreds of possible sellers to buy from, you need to learn how to use your time wisely, and asking questions over the phone is an efficient use of your time. You will be surprised by how much sellers will tell you.

After you talk to a seller, rank both his or her motivation and the potential profitability of the house on a scale of 1 to 10. A partial list of motivations appears on page 40. You will hear many other answers and can fit them into this list.

Use these scales to compare two or more houses directly and decide which one to pursue first.

Once you find a seller with a high motivation who owns a house that is desirable, stop looking and go buy the house!

LOOK FOR A SELLER WHO IS TRYING HARD TO SELL YOU HIS HOUSE

Every seller and every situation are different. You want to buy from a seller who needs to sell and who is trying hard to sell you his house as opposed to someone who is playing hard to get. If you find yourself trying to convince the person to sell to you, the seller is not as motivated as you are. Look for a cooperative attitude in a seller. A seller who avoids answering questions and won't make concessions is not ready to make you a good deal.

Another test that you can give a seller is to ask her to come to you. Before I go see a house in my town, I ask the seller to come to my office for a meeting. If she won't come, she is showing me that she is not motivated enough for me to make her an offer. If she doesn't show up, at least I know I have not wasted a lot of time.

Sellers will try to get you to come see them. As a test, you should offer to meet the seller. If you do not have an office, offer to meet in a safe place,

Seller's Motivation Scale
(10 is the highest motivation)

1 The seller wants to buy a new house when she sells.
2 The seller's kids are starting school next year, and the family wants to move to another school district.
3 The seller is expecting twins and needs a bigger house.
4 The seller's in-laws are moving in, and the family needs a bigger house.
5 The seller has bought a new house, and it closes in two weeks.
6 The seller has a new job in another town starting next week.
7 The seller's spouse has a new job in another town starting next week.
8 The seller is leaving town tomorrow and can't afford two payments.
9 The seller is months behind in his or her payments, and the foreclosure sale is next week.
10 The foreclosure sale is tomorrow, and the seller will pay you to buy their house and stop the foreclosure.

Potential House Profitability Scale
(10 is the most desirable)

1 Older, small house in poor repair, small lot, marginal neighborhood
2 Older family-size house, good repair, marginal neighborhood
3 Small house, small lot, marginal neighborhood
4 Newer family-size house, average-size lot, busy street
5 Older family-size house, good lot, average neighborhood
6 Newer family-size house, good lot, average neighborhood
7 Newer family-size house, good lot, great neighborhood
8 Older small house, great lot, great neighborhood
9 Newer small house, great lot, great neighborhood
10 Newer family-size house, great lot, great neighborhood

perhaps a bank lobby (convenient to you) or a coffee shop. If the seller does come, you will have won the first negotiation and learned something about his motivation.

One seller of an empty house called me from his new location, a three-hour drive away. He knew I bought houses and said that he wanted to sell me his house. I looked at the house and told him I was not interested in buying it because it would not make a good long-term investment. He said he wanted to sell it to me anyway and would drive over to meet me. He drove three hours and made me an offer I could not refuse. When sellers are ready to sell, they will send signals like driving three hours to sell their empty house.

There is no set formula for making offers. There is no rule that you make an offer after a certain number of hours or questions. Every seller is different. Always test the seller to see if he is ready to sell you the property.

The way to test is to ask questions and see how the seller responds. You can ask very direct questions, such as, "Are you ready to sell your house today?" or "Can you be out by this weekend?" These questions will also raise the seller's level of expectation—she will think that you are interested in buying and buying now!

You are, of course—but only if you can make a good deal.

If you ask those two questions, and the seller answers yes to both, then the seller is ready for you to make an offer.

Before you sit down with a seller to make an offer, *write down your strategy.* Use the worksheet shown in Figure 4.1 to gather current market information and to think through what you want to offer. Write down the most you are willing to pay for the house, the price you hope to buy it for, and the best price you can imagine buying it for. Write down the amount and terms of the financing you need to make the house a viable investment.

It's important to write down these figures. When you are making the offer, the seller may be a better negotiator than you are and will try to talk you into paying more for the property. You need a well-thought-out plan before you actually begin the exciting process of negotiation.

Successful buyers prepare and have a game plan before they make an offer. They anticipate the seller's response and plan a counteroffer. Like a chess player, a good negotiator thinks a move or two ahead. Like chess, your opponent sometimes surprises you, and when that happens, you need to step back and rethink your plan.

FIGURE 4.1   Buying Strategy Worksheet

House Address: _____

Date: _____

Sellers' names: _____

Other houses sold in the area:

Address: _____
Price: $_____   Date: _____
Address: _____
Price: $_____   Date: _____
Address: _____
Price: $_____   Date: _____

Other houses now on the market in the area:

Address: _____
Price: $_____   Date: _____
Address: _____
Price: $_____   Date: _____
Address: _____
Price: $_____   Date: _____

The estimated gross monthly rent the house will produce:
$_____

Estimated monthly expenses (taxes, insurance, maintenance):
$_____

Net amount available for payments: $_____

Highest price that you are willing to pay: $_____

FIGURE 4.1 Buying Strategy Worksheet (*continued*)

Your target price: $_____

The best price you can imagine: $_____

The first price you will offer: $_____

The largest down payment you can make: $_____

The first down payment you will offer: $_____

The amount of financing: $_____

The terms of the financing:

Interest rate: _____%   Term: _____ years   Payment: $_____

Your projected monthly cash flow: $_____

Personal property and other terms or conditions important to you
in this purchase:

_____

_____

5

KNOWING WHAT A HOUSE IS WORTH BEFORE YOU MAKE AN OFFER

When you are buying a high-dollar item, such as a house, you need to know what it is worth to you before you make an offer. You cannot predict what the seller will take for the property. The amount that a property will sell for can change every day. It is the price that a real buyer and the seller can agree on that particular day. Since both the seller's and buyer's situations can change in a heartbeat, the price that a property will sell for is unpredictable.

The property's value to you can be established. If you are trying to buy a property that produces a certain amount of cash flow or that has a good chance of appreciation in value because of its location, then you can put a price on the property that you would be willing to pay.

By researching recent sales of other properties in the immediate neighborhood that are comparable in quality and condition, you can learn what the property would sell for at a retail price. The retail price is the price that the property will sell for, given enough time (which is a long time in many markets) and exposure to the market by someone who is able to negotiate a sale. It is generally the price a competent Realtor will get for a seller given enough time.

You have heard that real estate is illiquid. A more accurate statement is that it takes time to liquidate real estate at a retail price.

At a wholesale price, real estate is liquid. I will buy a house and close on it in one or two days, giving the sellers cash for their equity, at a wholesale price. This is about the same amount of time it would take the seller to sell a stock and get cash.

What is the difference between retail and wholesale? It is different with different types of real estate, so let's focus on houses. If you are buying land or commercial property, it is much more difficult to determine what a property is really worth, and the difference between retail and wholesale can be much greater.

Even with houses, the difference between retail and wholesale is different in different price ranges. The lowest-priced housing in a community generally will be in poor repair and in neighborhoods with little potential for appreciation. Lenders are not fond of making loans on such properties, and, because of this, buyers are unable to obtain financing to buy these houses. This makes the lower price range less liquid. Although you can buy these houses at what looks like a bargain price, when you sell them, you may have to sell at a significant discount or finance the purchase for a buyer with poor credit.

Some investors buy these low-priced houses because they can rent them for a high rent compared with the price they paid for the house, but these houses will require a lot of management, and the owners will not benefit from the appreciation they might receive with higher-priced houses.

On the other end of the price range are the most expensive houses in your town. These are more illiquid and might sell for a 20, 30, or 40 percent discount because relatively few buyers want these houses.

Anyone who can afford to buy a very expensive house has other alternatives. These buyers can choose to buy less expensive houses, so the most expensive houses in your market also sell at a larger than normal discount if the seller is forced to sell in a hurry. This is a real opportunity for a buyer, but you must be able to afford to own the house until you can sell it at a retail price, and that could be a long time.

Houses in the middle ranges sell for closest to retail. This makes them more of a challenge to buy at wholesale prices, but it makes them safer investments in the long run. Since these houses frequently sell at retail prices, it is easier to determine their value. You can research recent sales through your public records (which can often be found online) or through the multiple-listing service records that any Realtor can provide for you.

Because these houses are more liquid, you can safely pay closer to a retail price, knowing that if you need to sell, you can get your money back in a reasonable period of time.

What is a wholesale price for an average house in a moderately priced neighborhood in your town? It depends on your market conditions. If there are a lot of willing buyers in your market, and lenders are willing to finance them, then a discount of 10 to 20 percent off the retail price is wholesale. It allows you to buy the house, hold it for a while, and then resell it for a profit.

There are holding costs to owning a house. An investor will rent a house as soon as possible to generate income to pay the cost of holding the house and will wait to resell until the house has appreciated. A speculator may buy a house and try to resell it immediately for a much smaller profit. Until she sells it, she must pay the holding costs, which are depleting her profits daily. Obviously, investing for the long run is a much more predictable way to make much more money with less risk.

If you are new to a market. How do you know how much to offer when you are buying a house? You can pay for an appraisal before you make an offer, but that is expensive, time consuming, and appraisers do get it wrong occasionally.

You can simply make a very low offer and see how the seller responds. One downside to this, if the property is listed, is that some brokers will refuse to present your offer or will present it in such a way that you don't even get a counteroffer. If another buyer is in the wings, the low offer may give them the contrast they need to get their higher offer accepted.

An alternative is learning to place a value on the property yourself. This is easier in a stable market but possible in any market. I teach students in my seminars to estimate a price that is within 10 percent (plus or minus) of the value. I recently bought a house that was worth about $145,000. My estimation of the value was a range of $125,000 to $150,000. An appraisal would have been in that range.

My first offer was $110,000 (a little under 10 percent below my lower figure) and we closed at $115,000 with favorable owner financing. An important part of the value of this deal was the owner financing, which allowed me to buy with a small down payment and have several hundred dollars a month in cash flow. I would not have paid $115,000 cash for the house. (See Normal Returns on Investment (ROI) on the next page.)

Part of the answer to the question "how much to pay?" depends on the direction of the market in your town. Your paper may report that prices are going up or down, but every town has many markets. Every street has a market. Some streets have many foreclosures or short sales, while others have none.

Different neighborhoods are different markets. While some streets have a lot of houses for sale or rent, others (in the same price range) may have none.

Which streets have the more stable prices? Another factor (rarely considered by appraisers or prognosticators) that influences value is the number of free and clear properties in a neighborhood. Find a street that is loaded with long-term residents and you will find many free-and-clear and high-equity properties. In addition to more stable prices you will find more owner financing opportunities on these streets.

Obviously a street loaded with free-and-clear properties will have few, if any, foreclosures, although a long-term owner in a hurry occasionally needs to discount the price to attract a buyer. This lack of distressed sales helps keep the prices up in these neighborhoods.

When credit is tight for potential homebuyers, many people who would like to buy a house can't qualify for a loan. As credit becomes more available, more buyers will return to the market to compete for the existing housing inventory. The National Association of Realtors reports the amount of inventory and the average time on the market in different markets. Get this information for your town from a local Realtor or look on the National Association of Realtors' website (www.realtor.org).

SHORT SALES AND FORECLOSURES ARE ALL DISTRESSED SALES

A distressed sale, a foreclosure or short sale, is not sold at a market price. Often the house being sold is not in good condition. It may need significant repairs just to make it livable.

When a street has only distressed sales, then the perception is that all houses have dropped in value. When the distressed inventory is gone, the prices of houses in good condition will return to "normal." What is "normal"? In a normal market a buyer can choose from existing houses in good repair or new inventory. The new inventory sells for the builder's cost plus his profit and buyers are willing to pay a premium for a new house that is available immediately. A comparable used house will sell for less. However, a well-maintained used home may be in a better location and that location may command a premium.

NORMAL RETURNS ON INVESTMENT (ROI)

In a normal market, a buyer of an investment house might expect a net return from rents in the 4 to 6 percent range. In a distressed market, houses sell for less and the net return from rentals is higher. In a distressed market, you might make 8 to 12 percent net return based on distressed prices.

This is higher than normal and is only possible because of the bargain prices, not high rents. The rental market is often less volatile than the sales market. Rents will drop in a recession, but not as much as prices in hard-hit markets.

Know the trends in the job market and the rental market in your town. When jobs and tenants are disappearing, you might make your best deals, but it is a risky time to buy.

When the job and rental markets show signs of improvement, you may have missed the bottom of the market, but there will still be plenty of good deals. It's much safer to buy when you know that you can find a good tenant than when you are uncertain about your ability to rent.

You don't want to lower your standards and rent to a marginal tenant. In a soft market, drop your rents to attract (or maybe steal) a good tenant.

THREE WAYS TO EVALUATE A HOUSE BEFORE YOU MAKE AN OFFER

Fair market value is the price that a willing buyer will pay a willing seller in an arm's length transaction. Of course, the credit market has a lot to do with how much a buyer will pay. When the credit is freely available, prices will be higher than in a tight credit market.

Market Sales

Current sales are the primary source of "comps" or comparable sales used by appraisers to establish value in a residential appraisal in a normal market. If the market is heavily loaded with distressed sales, then you actually have two markets. There is a market for distressed sales and another for sales of non-distressed (in good condition both physically and financially) houses.

In a typical market, a distressed sale would not be considered as a comparable for a well-maintained house sold in an arm's length transaction. During a recession, distressed sales can be the majority of the sales, making it difficult for an appraiser to establish values.

Bruce Norris, a successful California investor overcomes this when selling by hiring an appraiser to research and find a number of comparable sales of rehabbed or other houses in good condition. They then share these comparable sales with the lender's appraiser. This helps the lender's appraiser and helps the buyer and the seller close the transaction.

When Determining What to Offer, Look for the Trend in a Neighborhood

When looking for trends in neighborhood house prices, the challenge is finding houses that are "equal." Every house has a unique lot, design, features, neighbors, and has been cared for differently. The best way I know to compare values in a neighborhood is to compare sales of the same house, accounting for renovations, if any, and changes in the neighborhood. Look for sales ten to twenty years apart to lap a market cycle. This takes local knowledge, and appraisers do not have the time to make this level of comparison.

Appraisers have to produce an appraisal report in a few hours, so they rely heavily on sales figures from the public records. Although they try to find comparable properties, they can't take the time to drive every street and research every property to see if it is indeed a lot like the house that they are trying to appraise.

Look for Signs of Improving Streets

Look for streets where others are fixing up houses to rent or to sell. The average sale price will climb dramatically on these streets in a short time. Should you acquire a distressed property, the next step is to fix it up. I have purchased and renovated a number of houses. Here are some typical numbers: purchase price $100,000; repairs $40,000; sale price $180,000. You can see the effect on the neighborhood and on comparable sales when a distressed property is turned into a retail property.

Notice Over- or Under-Improved
Houses on the Street

In a hot market some builders and rehabbers build or remodel houses and make them too expensive for the neighborhood. They buy cheaper lots and build houses that are too big or too fancy for the market. These over-improved houses often sell for less than what it cost to build them. This will depress prices of the over-improved properties on these streets. Other streets have smaller (typically older) houses built on good lots. These houses are likely to be expanded or simply razed as the lot value becomes more than the value of the improvements.

Pay Attention to the Financial
State of the Owners

Are there a lot of Realtor signs advertising short sales (or just a lot of signs)? Short sales and foreclosures are an indication of the amount of debt (too much) on the properties. These properties will sell below the market, depressing the process for a while. If you are buying on a street with many foreclosures or short sales, calculate your best offer, and then reduce it by another 20 percent.

Look for Long-Term Residents

One fun part about walking through neighborhoods and talking to the owners is finding someone who has lived in the same house for fifty years and knows the history and all about the current residents. They notice owners coming and going, know who has a growing family and know who is close to moving out.

A lot of long-term residents speaks well of a neighborhood. Neighborhoods can go downhill, even with long-term owners, but I prefer to own in a neighborhood where people want to stay, not in one where they want to get out. Talking to people will give you the inside track on what is happening on a street.

The Income Approach

Another approach used to establish a property's value is the income approach. Although with residential real estate this approach is typically given less weight, but it can help you establish what to pay for a house.

Houses are unique among income-producing real estate. Some property has only an investment value. The only reason you would buy a commercial or industrial building is to generate an income, so their value is primarily based on the income that they produce. A lower income results in a lower value.

A house has value separate from its income. A house is valuable to a user, and often this value is higher than the value it has as a producer of income.

In a "normal" market, a median-priced house will rent for enough to give an investor a 4 to 6 percent return. This is the return after expenses, but before income taxes. This also disregards the effect of leverage. When you finance part of your purchase, your rate of return will be amplified.

In order to compare apples with apples, compare incomes as if the houses were free and clear. When you can buy a house that will give you a much higher return than 4 to 6 percent, you have reinforcement that you are buying at a bargain price. Of course, less expensive houses often produce more gross cash flow, but they may also attract higher-maintenance tenants, which leads to higher maintenance costs. Be careful to compare houses in the same general price range when comparing net incomes.

The Reproduction Cost Approach

A third way to determine value is to calculate what it would cost to reproduce a property. Of course, a reproduced house would be a new one, so an adjustment for the age and condition of the house would be used to adjust the value.

In the price range that most of us buy houses for investment, the cost of construction would be in a fairly tight range. Different construction materials, block or brick instead of frame might have an impact on both cost and marketability. Some builders have good reputations for building a quality house while others build as cheaply as possible. These factors affect the long-term maintenance cost of a house and its value today.

The part of the cost that is less consistent is the cost of not just the land but also the site preparation. If a lot is low, it may require tens of thousands of dollars in fill, compacting, and grading before you can build. Likewise, if drainage is an issue, you can spend an extraordinary amount installing a septic system. Additionally, if you don't have access to a central water system, a well can be a big expense.

These items can be expensive but add little value to the house, since every house needs working plumbing and a building pad. Landscaping is not a big factor when buying a rental, but it can be expensive. Don't put a lot of value on landscaping and site improvements.

USING THE THREE APPROACHES
TO DETERMINE HOW MUCH TO OFFER

In a rising market, the market approach has advantages over the income and reproduction approaches. Rents sometimes lag behind price increases, so the income approach can be low. And move-in-ready houses, with mature landscaping in an established neighborhood, will sell for a premium over a house to be built, so your existing houses may be worth more than reproduction costs.

In a falling market, the income approach is a good gauge. If you can buy a house and get an 8 to 10 percent return on your money when banks are paying a fraction of that on savings accounts, it's a good deal. Combine that with the opportunity to buy with a low interest rate loan and you have a license to steal.

YOUR PERCEPTION OF THE FUTURE
WILL INFLUENCE YOUR OFFER

Because your perception of your market will influence how much you offer, the seller's perception of the future will influence how he responds to your offer. Find a seller who thinks the market is still going down, and your chances of making a good deal go up. The public is always a day late when it comes to recognizing the top or bottom of a market.

6

KNOWING HOW YOU ARE GOING TO PAY FOR A HOUSE BEFORE YOU BUY

Before you make an offer to buy a house, you need to have a plan to pay for it. Your tenants can repay the money that you borrow if you pay a bargain price and borrow on better-than-market terms. The first step to making a profitable deal is to figure out how much income your tenants will generate.

You do not set the rent on a house; the market sets the rent. Some landlords try to rent their property for an amount equal to their loan payments. The tenants don't care how much your loan payments are; they will pay the least amount of rent they can for the best house they decide they can afford. Tenants will compare the houses on the market and rent the one that is the best deal.

To determine how much rent you can expect to collect, you need to study your market. Good information is available because landlords advertise their houses on line and in your newspaper every week.

HOW MUCH CAN YOUR POTENTIAL TENANTS AFFORD TO PAY?

To determine the amount of rent you can collect, conduct a rent survey of your competing landlords. Identify your target neighborhoods and your price range for desired rent. Check rents on online sites that list rentals in your town, like Craigslist, and look for rental ads in your local paper.

Then look for houses advertised for rent in your price ranges and, if possible, in your target neighborhoods.

Once you've found a few listings, call the landlord and ask the questions any potential renter would ask (see below), noting his or her answers.

1. Have you rented the house?
2. How big are the house and yard?
3. Has the house be updated?
4. What appliances come with the house?
5. Is the yard fenced?
6. Is it on a busy street?
7. How much is the rent?
8. Will you accept kids and pets?
9. Is there a limit to how many people can live in the house?
10. How much is the security deposit?
11. How long must the lease be?
12. How long has the house been empty?

You cannot assume that all of the answers are true, but a smart landlord will be truthful. The answers are easy to check by looking at the house.

You want to sort through the responses and separate the smart landlords (those who are charging a reasonable rent and security deposit) from the others (those who are willing to rent to anyone).

A landlord who has low standards for tenants or who will rent to too many people, such as six college students, can charge more than market rate. After the bad tenant moves out and the landlord makes repairs to the house, he will net far less rent.

Likewise, some landlords will rent without requiring a last month's rent or reasonable security deposit. They too can charge above-market rent, because they will let a tenant who has little money move in. These tenants often fall behind on their rent immediately because they don't have any money!

Surprisingly, many landlords will not answer the phone or respond to an inquiry when they are paying a lot of money to support an empty house.

Prepare a chart like Table 6.1, and record the information you obtain when talking to the landlords. Next, go see the houses that have rented and the houses that are still for rent. Make notes about the neighborhood and

Table 6.1 Landlord Survey

Date	Address	Phone Number	Size	Rent	Last Month's Rent	Security Deposit	Length of Stay Required	Kids/Pets (Y/N)	Has It Rented? (Y/N)	How Much
1.				$	$	$				$
2.				$	$	$				$
3.				$	$	$				$
4.				$	$	$				$
5.				$	$	$				$
6.				$	$	$				$
7.				$	$	$				$
8.				$	$	$				$
9.				$	$	$				$
10.				$	$	$				$
11.				$	$	$				$
12.				$	$	$				$
13.				$	$	$				$
14.				$	$	$				$
15.				$	$	$				$
16.				$	$	$				$
17.				$	$	$				$
18.				$	$	$				$
19.				$	$	$				$
20.				$	$	$				$

the condition of the houses and start learning about your competition. Many landlords do not buy good properties, nor do they maintain the houses well. Try to buy in better neighborhoods, and keep your houses in good condition. This will reduce your vacancies because your houses will be the first to rent.

Now that you have a good idea of what your competition is and have studied the amount of rents, deposits, and number of vacancies in your target neighborhood, you can make a good estimate of the amount of rent you can expect to collect.

RENTS AND PRICES GO UP, BUT AT DIFFERENT TIMES

One big benefit of investing in houses is that your rents will increase significantly over the years, whereas your loan payments can remain the same until the loan is paid off. Rents tend to increase at the same rate as prices, but in different years.

In a hot real estate market, when prices are increasing rapidly, rents may be stable and may even drop. This is a result of low interest rates, which allow renters to buy houses and encourage builders to build. When interest rates are low and house prices are rising rapidly, many investors also buy houses and rent them. This increased supply of rental houses, coupled with many renters becoming homeowners, can keep rents low.

When interest rates rise, fewer renters can qualify to buy, and fewer investors buy houses for rental. These factors combine to cause a tight rental market, and rents rise as tenants compete for fewer houses. Understanding and recognizing these cycles in your town is important. Although rents will increase in the long run, these cycles often last several years at a time (see Figure 6.1).

Notice that house prices increase in some years, are flat in others, and even occasionally drop. Although, when they drop, they rarely drop below the earlier low and when they recover, they often surpass the previous high.

This result is more pronounced in markets prone to big swings in prices. In a market where house prices just creep up every year, it will appear that rents and prices go up together.

Although rents and prices can experience short-term dips, in the long run both will increase with inflation. These dips will be larger in higher-priced properties.

FIGURE 6.1 The Impact of Interest Rates on House
Prices and Rents

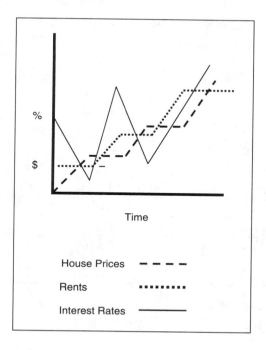

HOW MUCH WILL YOU SPEND
TO OPERATE THE HOUSE?

Every house will cost a different amount to operate. Well-designed and well-built homes that have been maintained and are well situated on good lots will be far less expensive to maintain than poorly designed and built homes on troublesome lots.

You want to buy a house that will produce the most income in relation to what it will cost to operate. You might think that a very small house that would be less expensive to maintain would be best. But you want a house that is large enough to attract a good long-term tenant, and you want it in a neighborhood that will reward you with appreciation.

Use the worksheet in Figure 6.2 to project the income you will have to repay a loan.

This assumes that you will manage the property yourself. If you plan to pay a manager, plug in his fee.

FIGURE 6.2   Calculating the Income a House Will Produce

Here are actual figures for a house in my town:

Gross rent: $1,500 to $1,600

Using the lower end of the rent range: $1,500

	Annual	**Monthly**
Rent	$18,000	$1,500
Operating expenses:		
Property taxes	$2,400	$200
Casualty insurance	$480	$40
Liability insurance	$60	$5
Repairs and maintenance	$3,600	$300
Total expenses	$6,540	$545
Net rent available for loan payments	$11,460	$955

HOW MUCH CAN YOU BORROW AND REPAY WITH THE RENT YOUR TENANTS PAY?

Interest rates change constantly. When you buy a house for investment, try to borrow on a long-term, fixed-interest-rate loan. Then you will be able to predict your cash flow accurately and benefit as rents increase and your loan payment stays constant.

Table 6.2 shows you the amount that you can afford to repay with the rent you collect at different interest rates. Use this chart as a guide when you are calculating how much you can afford to repay with the net rents that a property would generate.

Then calculate the exact payment any loan would have using a financial calculator. You can buy one at any large office supply store or download an app onto your phone.

Study Table 6.2 so that you become familiar with how much you can borrow to buy houses that produce certain amounts of net rent (rent after

Table 6.2   How Much Can you Repay with Different Rents?

Amount of Net Rent (Loan Payment)	Interest Rate	Loan Amount	Term
$500	6%	$83,385	30 years
	8%	$68,142	30 years
	10%	$56,975	30 years
$600	6%	$100,075	30 years
	8%	$81,770	30 years
	10%	$68,370	30 years
$700	6%	$116,754	30 years
	8%	$95,398	30 years
	10%	$79,766	30 years
$800	6%	$133,433	30 years
	8%	$109,026	30 years
	10%	$91,160	30 years
$900	6%	$150,112	30 years
	8%	$122,655	30 years
	10%	$102,556	30 years
$1,000	6%	$167,626	30 years
	8%	$137,192	30 years
	10%	$114,900	30 years
$1,250	6%	$209,531	30 years
	8%	$171,490	30 years
	10%	$143,625	30 years
$1,500	6%	$251,438	30 years
	8%	$205,788	30 years
	10%	$172,350	30 years
$2,000	6%	$335,251	30 years
	8%	$274,384	30 years
	10%	$229,800	30 years
$3,000	6%	$502,876	30 years
	8%	$411,576	30 years
	10%	$334,701	30 years

expenses). Identify the range of rents in your town, and remember these numbers. Now you can make an offer knowing that the rents will cover your payments if you borrow on terms with these payments.

ALWAYS BORROW FOR THE LONGEST AVAILABLE TERM

Using the word *always* will cause you to struggle with this idea, and this is good. Can we agree that a loan with a lower payment is a safer loan for you to owe? If you had to lower your rents to keep your house full, the longer-term loan would give you the lowest possible payment.

When you borrow to buy property, the longer-term loan allows you to borrow more money. You can buy a property with less of your cash invested. Although thirty-year loans are common, as rates rise, longer-term loans may be available.

When you are beginning to invest, you need to use your available cash sparingly. Buying with a low down payment is a better strategy than using much of your cash for a down payment. If your house sits empty for two months before you rent it, you will need cash for payments.

Even with a thirty-year amortization schedule, you are paying a considerable amount of principal each month. Compare the thirty-year amortizing loan with an interest-only payment (see Table 6.3).

You can pay off a loan before its due date. However, when you are still in the property-acquisition mode and can use your cash to buy a house that will make you a 20 percent or higher annual return, why would you want to use that cash to pay off a loan that is only costing you 6, 8, or even 10 percent?

After you have acquired all the properties that you want, you can shift gears and begin to pay off your debt. Owning free-and-clear real estate is a good strategy.

When you begin, focus on buying properties with long-term financing. After you own many properties with long-term loans, you can then use your cash flow to begin reducing your debt. How long does it take to pay off a thirty-year loan? About ten minutes. You just write a check for the balance. Just because you borrow on thirty-year terms does not mean that you have to wait thirty years to own your houses free and clear. Later you will learn how to pay off your debt and get your houses free and clear in far less than thirty years.

Table 6.3 Even Thirty-Year Loans Have Large Principal Payments

Amount of Payment	Interest Rate	Loan Amount	Term	Interest-Only Payment	Principal Payment
$500	6%	$83,385	30 years	$416.92	$83.08
	8%	$68,142	30 years	$454.28	$45.72
	10%	$56,975	30 years	$474.79	$25.20
$1,000	6%	$167,626	30 years	$838.13	$161.87
	8%	$137,192	30 years	$914.61	$85.38
	10%	$114,900	30 years	$957.50	$42.50
$2,000	6%	$335,251	30 years	$1,676.25	$323.74
	8%	$274,384	30 years	$1,829.22	$171.77
	10%	$229,800	30 years	$1,915.00	$85.00
$3,000	6%	$502,876	30 years	$2,514.38	$485.62
	8%	$411,576	30 years	$2,743.84	$256.16
	10%	$334,701	30 years	$2,789.18	$210.82

SCHAUB'S 10/10/10 RULE FOR BUYING AT A PROFIT

My 10/10/10 rule for buying a house states that when you buy, you make no more than a 10 percent down payment, pay no more than 10 percent interest, and buy at least 10 percent under the market. This rule of thumb will help you to put together offers to buy houses that will pay for themselves.

1. *Pay no more than 10 percent down.* A smaller down payment is better for you in several ways.

First, you have more liquidity. In the event that you have to resell the house quickly, it will be easier to find a buyer who can put 10 percent down than one with a larger down payment.

Second, you have less risk because you have less to lose. The lender has more to lose when you borrow using the property as the collateral for your loan.

Third, you can buy more houses if you use your cash sparingly.

When you make a smaller down payment, your rate of return on your investment increases. Suppose that you put $30,000 down and buy a house that produces $2,000 a year in cash flow plus $4,000 a year in appreciation and principal paydown. Your profit, expressed as a ratio of the annual profit the property produces divided by the amount of money you have invested, is $6,000/$30,000, or 20 percent. This is your rate of return on your investment.

If you bought the same house with $10,000 down, your cash flow would drop as your loan payment increased. Suppose that you had zero cash flow and the same $4,000 in appreciation and principal paydown. In this case, your rate of return would be $4,000/$10,000, or 40 percent. By doubling the return on your investment, you cut in half the time it will take you to reach your financial goals.

2. *Pay no more than 10 percent interest* on the money you borrow to finance. House interest rates vary with time—even when rates are low, some investors are paying more than 10 percent to finance property. Whatever the interest rate a bank is charging, you can borrow at a lower rate from sellers and other investors.

Since interest is the largest component of your payment, the rate of interest that you pay determines in large part how much profit you will make on the house. Work hard to get the best possible interest rate when you borrow.

3. *Buy at least 10 percent below the market.* Buying at a below-market price makes you a profit the day you buy. In addition, it reduces the amount of money that you have to borrow to buy the house, which increases your cash flow.

It also makes the deal safer and more liquid. If you needed to sell in a hurry, you could sell to someone else at a below-market price and get your down payment back and hopefully a little profit.

Thus, 10/10/10 is the worst deal you should make. You should make every attempt to buy a house with a lower down payment, borrow at a lower interest rate, or buy it for less than 10 percent below the market.

If you bought a $200,000 rental house in my town today using 10/10/10, your purchase would look like this:

Market value:	$200,000 to $225,000
Your purchase price:	$180,000 (10 percent below the market)

Your down payment: $18,000 (10 percent of $180,000)

Your loan: $162,000 (thirty-year fixed-rate at 5 percent) This rate will vary with the market.

Your loan payment: $870

The monthly rent: $1,500

Monthly operating expenses: $545*

Net operating income: $955

Less loan payment: $870 (first-month principal reduction on the loan is $195)

*The operating expenses on a rental house will vary with the age and condition of the house, your ability to manage the property, and your local property tax and insurance rates. Houses in good repair that are well built can have lower maintenance expenses.

Calculating the net return on your down payment:

	Monthly	Annual
Cash flow:	$85	$1,020
Loan amortization:	$195	$2,340 (The first year)
Total:	$280	$3,360

Net annual return on your down payment 3,360/18,000 = 18.6%.

Note: This rate of return does not include appreciation. The financing is a key factor. If you have to pay a higher interest rate, try to negotiate a longer term with lower payments.

Never use potential appreciation to talk yourself into buying a property. Buy one that gives you an acceptable return on your investment without appreciation, and then the appreciation will make a good deal even better.

YOUR FIRST $18,000 GROWS TO $194,000 IN A DECADE

If you hold this house until the house doubles in value ($400,000) and it takes ten years, the loan balance would be $139,016. If you sell the house for $400,000, you would net before taxes about $260,000. If you can invest $18,000 for ten years and receive $260,000 at the end of that time, you have earned an annual compounded rate of return of just over 30 percent. If it takes fifteen years, your rate of return is 19.4 percent. If it takes twenty years your rate of return is 14.2 percent. This does not include the cash flow that the property produces that we discussed above, nor does it account for tax benefits or costs.

This rate of return is as high as it is because of two factors: First, the prudent use of leverage that allowed you to buy an asset worth $200,000 with an $18,000 cash investment that then would pay for itself. Second, the continuous investment of your money in a profitable asset for a long period of time. This combination of "positive leverage" and a long-term strategy allows investors to accumulate millions of dollars in net worth in a fraction of their lifetime.

FORMING YOUR BUYING STRATEGY

Before you make an offer, take the time to really know the neighborhood. Walk, don't drive, up and down the street and the streets around the house. Meet the neighbors. Notice what's going on in the neighborhood. Are there a lot of houses for sale or for rent? Are all the houses well maintained? Do you notice any empty houses?

Look for other opportunities. Sometimes you will find a better deal by walking and talking to others who live in the neighborhood. Ask the neighbors if they know of anyone who is selling. You will be surprised at how much the neighbors know and how much they will tell you.

Research both recent sales and properties now on the market to get a good feel for prices. Rather than trying to establish an exact price for a house you are looking at, give yourself a range of prices, for example, $200,000 to $240,000. Now you know that if you can buy at the low end of that range or below, it's a good deal.

SET A MINIMUM ACCEPTABLE PROFIT FOR THE HOUSE

There is some risk every time you buy a house. You will invest a considerable amount of time when you buy, rent, and sell a house. Although you are not guaranteed a profit, you should buy at a price that gives you a high probability of making a profit.

The more expensive the house you invest in, the larger your minimum profit should be. You take a smaller risk buying a less expensive house. It is easier to rent and easier to resell. You take a greater risk when you buy a more expensive house. You need to buy it further below the market to compensate yourself for that risk. If you had to resell it immediately, you would have to discount the price to get rid of it quickly.

The difference between your minimum profit and my advice to buy a house at least 10 percent below the market is the result of combining a discounted price with favorable financing that allows the house to produce a profit from rents. A more expensive house will have less of its profit from rental income and more from a bargain purchase.

Following are some examples of house prices and minimum profits. This is not a science. These numbers should make you consider the relationship between the risks you are taking and the price you should pay for a house. You need to adjust the discount to account for the quality and location of the house and the market for houses at the time. You may decide that there is little risk in buying a higher-quality house in a strong market, especially if you can buy it with favorable financing.

House Value	Minimum Profit
$50,000 to $80,000	$10,000
$80,000 to $120,000	$15,000
$120,000 to $150,000	$20,000
$150,000 to $180,000	$25,000
$180,000 to $210,000	$30,000
$210,000 to $240,000	$35,000
$240,000 to $270,000	$40,000
$270,000 to $300,000	$45,000
$300,000+	$50,000

7

WHAT MAKES SOME DEBT DANGEROUS AND HOW TO BORROW SAFELY

I don't believe that all debt is dangerous. However, I do believe that the leading cause of going broke is borrowing money you can't pay back. Those who have gone broke, filed for bankruptcy relief, or had a foreclosure are rightfully fearful of debt.

There is good debt, and there is bad debt. Debt used to buy an investment that can repay that debt is valuable to a real estate investor. Debt used to support a lifestyle you cannot afford is the road to bankruptcy.

Consumer debt is typically bad debt. If you can't afford to pay cash for a new car or a vacation, drive your old one until you save up to buy one you like better, or have a staycation. If you have a car loan or consumer debt, make a plan to pay it off as a first step to becoming an investor.

FIVE REASONS CONSUMER DEBT WILL KEEP YOU POOR

1. The interest rates are high.
2. The term is short.
3. The payments are high in relation to how much you owe.

4. The interest is not deductible.
5. Whatever you bought is going down in value.

You can now get a seven-year car loan that may outlast the car you buy.

Contrast that with a house mortgage. The lender has a house as security for her loan and you probably made a down payment. Therefore, your interest rate will be lower and the term long enough to allow you to rent the house and have immediate cash flow. The interest is deductible, and the loan is secured by an asset that might grow in value.

A 70 percent loan ($160,000) on a $200,000 rental house is safer than a $10,000 credit card "loan." The house, if managed well, should produce enough rental income to repay the loan. Things you buy with your credit card rarely produce any income.

A CREDIT CARD CAN BE A VALUABLE TOOL

Credit cards used for a business purpose are valuable. A landlord can pay his contractors, buy needed materials, and maybe even pay insurance and tax bills. As long as he pays his credit card bill when due, he can get an interest-free loan from the time he charges until he pays his bill.

It's a business tool, and your business plan should include paying it on time every month. Otherwise you will start paying interest and, even worse, deferring payments of your current expenses. This is a sign of serious danger in your business or investments.

Personal credit cards can be a valuable tool, as long as you have the discipline and money to pay your bill on time each month. Not paying on time is a sign of financial danger.

UNINTENTIONAL DEBT

Life is full of unexpected surprises, not all of them good. Personal debt due to an accident or health and family issues is nothing you can plan for. However, you have a few options. One might be to renegotiate for lower payments. Another might be to negotiate a discount, if you can pay it off in a shorter time.

If you owe a hospital, it will certainly work out a payment plan that you can afford. The hospital may also be open to discounted payments. Ask anyone you owe if they can give you a discount if you could pay them early, and then make a plan to pay them.

Although this may seem out of reach today, in the future you may be able to sell an investment house and make a large enough payment to wipe out this debt. In the meantime, you could use the rental income that the house produces to begin to pay down the debt.

UNDERSTANDING WHY SOME REAL ESTATE LOANS ARE DANGEROUS

Not all real estate loans are created equal. In fact, some have little risk while others are extraordinary dangerous.

These are the factors that make a loan dangerous:

1. Short Term

A five-year loan may sound safe, but five years is not long enough for most markets to go through a full cycle. If interest rates are higher five years from now, you may have a hard time refinancing or selling at a good price.

Time is your friend as an investor. Plan to hold your investment properties until they double, and get a loan long enough to ensure that you can hold the property that long. Ten years is the shortest loan that I recommend for a real estate investment, and longer than ten is safer still.

2. A Variable Interest Rate or Payment

Although you may be able to get an initial lower interest rate with a variable-interest-rate loan, you are betting that rates will drop or stay low. A thirty-year, fixed-rate loan has an interest rate that has been adjusted to compensate for the risk of the longer term. If the cash flow from the house that you are buying will not make the payments on the thirty-year, fixed-rate loan, then you are speculating.

If you get a fixed-payment, thirty-year loan, as you raise your rents, you get a raise. With a variable-rate loan, your payments may increase in a market where rents are dropping.

Don't gamble, invest. Finance houses that you buy with long-term, fixed-rate loans. If everything goes according to your plan, you can pay them off early. If rates jump up, then you won't risk losing your houses.

3. Negative Amortizing Loans

These loans have payments that are less than interest only. At first look, they may seem like a great deal, since with lower than normal payments you would have more cash flow. But that's not the complete picture.

As you are paying less than interest only, your loan has a growing principal balance. In addition, you may be paying a higher interest rate in return for the low payments. You could end up owing more than the house is worth.

4. Loans Requiring Personal Guarantees

When you personally guarantee to pay a debt, the lender has all of your personal assets (not protected by law) at its disposal to satisfy your debt. Should the house you borrow against drop in value and go into foreclosure, and should the lender not recover its loan balance, the lender can take your bank account or other property that you own.

Most borrowers do not realize this. In states where trust deeds and trustee sales are common, banks typically do not pursue other assets of the debtor, but they can and have. In mortgage states, lenders routinely get deficiency judgments and pursue other assets the borrower has to recover their loan plus the costs of foreclosure.

If you just have one house and not many other assets, the lender will probably just write off the deficiency and not pursue you. However, if you own several houses with equity, then the lender may well go after your other houses to recover its money and costs.

The next time you borrow from a bank, read the paperwork that it makes you sign to get the money. You will notice that it heavily favors the bank. If you plan to acquire a large amount of real estate equity, every loan you get from a bank will put that equity at risk if you can't make your payment on the loan.

Investors with bank loans lost their property due to this cross liability when they failed to make payments on one loan. They would lose one house, then the bank would come after another and on and on until the investor's houses were all gone. You will not be able to borrow once a bank starts foreclosing on your property.

Learn to finance with nonrecourse loans and reduce your risk of loss during a recession.

5. Borrowing Against the Wrong Collateral

The best collateral for a loan would be a property that is easy to sell and that can rent for more than enough to make the payments on the loan.

Properties that are hard to sell are often older, need work, or are in declining neighborhoods. In addition, some houses are just strange and don't appeal to many buyers. A one-bedroom house or a five-bedroom house both have limited appeal. In our town we have a house that looks like Noah's Ark. It is fun to look at but hard to sell.

Buy conventional-looking houses in well-maintained neighborhoods, and if you have to sell in a hurry you will be able to command a higher price.

Be sensitive to the ratio between the price of the house and the rent it will generate. Buy houses that will produce enough income to pay the expenses and repay your loan. In more expensive markets, buying on creative terms or with a larger down payment may be necessary to avoid having negative cash flow.

Early in my career I bought a number of older, less-expensive houses in the path of progress. Thirty years later, these houses are still in the path of progress. Because they are older and destined for demolition someday, they are a challenge to manage.

When I tried to sell these properties, I found that my tenants could not afford to buy and that my only market was other investors. They could not get bank loans, so I had to sell with owner financing to get rid of the properties.

Rules for Borrowing Safely

1. Buy properties that produce enough rent to pay the expenses and repay the loan.
2. Buy properties that are relatively easy to manage and easy to sell.
3. Avoid personal liability on any high-risk loan.
4. Borrow with the longest term possible—you can always pay it off early.

USING LEVERAGE WISELY

Leverage lets you do things that are impossible without it. You can lift a very heavy object, for instance a car, with a simple jack. A six-year-old who weighs fifty pounds can balance her two-hundred-pound father on a properly positioned seesaw.

In real estate, you can manage fifty or more houses without employees using systems that allow you to delegate, as I teach in my management course.

These systems allow you to leverage your time. Or you can start with $10,000 and acquire a million dollars or more in property without ever borrowing from a bank.

Leverage also has its ugly side. Anyone who has been upside down with a loan balance greater than the property value knows the pain of leverage gone bad. Anyone who has purchased a property with negative cash flow has paid for a lesson far more expensive than a seminar.

Leverage can lead to a fortune or bankruptcy. Here is the most important thing to know about leverage: *some loans are far more dangerous than others, even if they are the same amount and have the same terms.*

Millions of borrowers lost their property because they borrowed from the wrong lenders, lenders who immediately sold their loans. Other investors survived and even prospered with the same amount of debt.

The losers were encouraged to borrow by lenders who had no concept of the risk of borrowing. Bankers used to understand risk, and they would refuse to lend to those who probably could not repay. Today, the people making the loans are commissioned salespeople, not bankers.

Before you ever borrow again, take the responsibility for making the decision to borrow. Don't let a salesperson talk you into a loan you don't need or may not be able to repay. Make the decision to borrow based on your research and knowledge of the property and the income that it will produce.

SCHAUB'S LAWS OF LEVERAGE

Leverage Can Increase or Decrease Your Cash Flow

How can borrowing possibly increase your cash flow? Let's say that you have $100,000 to use to buy property. You can buy one house with the $100,000 that will produce $8,000 net annual income ($666 a month), or an 8 percent return.

What if, instead of buying just one house, you decided to buy four houses, each with $25,000 down and you were able to get four $75,000, 6 percent thirty-year loans? The payment on each loan would be $449.66 (call it $450) a month. Now, each of your four houses would have cash flow of $666 per month less the $450 payment, or $216 per month. Your net spendable income would be $864 (4 × 216). That is substantially more than the $666 one house would produce. In addition, the four loans would pay down approximately $304 per month the first year, with principal payments increasing every year.

Together the income and principal paydown total $1,168 a month compared to $666 a month if you owned one house free and clear.

Negative Leverage Reduces Your Cash Flow

"Negative leverage" occurs when a loan reduces your profit on a property. Using the same four houses mentioned above, change the interest rate to 9 percent and the payments to $603.47. Now your spendable income on the four houses is only ($666 − $603) = $63 a month, or a total of $252. This is far less than the $666 a month you could realize from one free-and-clear house. Of course, in an appreciating market owning four houses will make you more money than if you were to only own one house.

The amount of your payment is the key here. A higher interest rate will normally increase your payment but a shorter term can too.

These are all before-tax examples. Beginning investors often pay little, if any, tax. If you happen to be in a high tax bracket, you may want to use leverage to lower your tax burden. Don't confuse negative leverage with tax shelter. You will still have more after-tax income with positive leverage. Paying more interest to pay less in taxes is faulty thinking. Would you want to pay more to your plumber next year and have bigger deductions? Of course not, and you don't want to pay more interest to your lender, either.

Leverage Can Increase or Decrease Your Risk

Does more leverage increase your risk? Is a 90 percent loan more danger-ous than a 70 percent loan? It's easy to say yes, because normally the larger loan would have larger payments, thus more risk. But, from a different per-spective, with which loan do you have more to lose if disaster strikes and you lose the property? Obviously, the answer is the smaller loan.

Lower payments give you the ability to reduce your rents in tough times and still survive, thus making your debt safer. A loan with lower payments would reduce your risk. However, if you could not make your payments, a lender would rather foreclose a 70 percent loan, because the lender has a better chance of recovering its money instead of the house.

Therefore, an investor with a loan of 90 percent is in a better negotiating position should he have trouble making the payments because of a downturn in the economy. Combine this idea with avoiding personal liability on a loan and the borrower is in a much stronger negotiating position with a very small equity.

HOW THE TYPE OF COLLATERAL IMPACTS YOUR RISK

Some properties are much easier to sell at a near-retail price than others. This is *liquidity*, or the ability to get most or all of your money back from an investment quickly. Note that there are two important points—speed and recovering your money. Securities salespeople brag that stocks and bonds have liquidity, meaning you can sell them quickly. Of course, you can sell some real estate quickly (hold an auction), but the amount that you recover will depend on what type of property you own.

When banks curtail their lending, they stop lending on the hardest to sell properties first. Raw land, commercial and office buildings, and small investment properties are the first to be eliminated by the bankers. Owner-occupied single-family houses are the bankers' best collateral, so buyers can often get house loans when all other loans disappear.

If you are going to be stuck with a property during a recession, you don't want to be stuck with property that cannot be financed. If you have to sell to a cash buyer during a downturn, the price you get may be a small fraction of the property's actual value. A great time to buy is a lousy time to sell.

WHOM YOU OWE MATTERS

Banks and other institutions are harder to deal with than individuals. When you deal with an individual, a seller, or an investor, you are talking about their money. If someone's personal funds are at risk or if they can receive money that is owed to them sooner, they are generally very interested in talking.

At a bank, you are talking with an employee who is much more interested in keeping his job than helping you, even if it is in the bank's best interest to work with you.

As many builders and developers learned the hard way, if your bank goes broke, it may cause you to go broke. A builder or developer with a bank commitment to fund a project loses his ability to borrow if the bank goes broke. This generally happens during an economic downturn, so another bank loan is not available. That leaves the developer stuck with a partially finished project that has very little value.

Investors who have loans with "their" bank would face a similar problem, should their bank fail. Their loans will be acquired by another lender that will be difficult to negotiate with if the borrowers have a problem.

Consider the difference if you have loans with sellers or with investors instead of a bank. The seller or investor generally wants her money back, not the property. She will renegotiate the terms of a loan to allow you to survive a downturn if you have a plan to repay her eventually.

What you need in a downturn is an extension of time to pay. Markets recover eventually, so if you can negotiate an extension with your lender, you can survive and eventually repay the loan.

A MAJOR ADVANTAGE OF OWNER FINANCING

When you buy with owner financing, you can avoid personal liability for the debt. Therefore, if you cannot make the payments, you can give the property back to the seller without the fear of having the liability for the debt. This is not the case with institutional loans. If you have borrowed cash from a bank to buy a property and do not pay it back, the bank can take other assets that you have in order to satisfy your obligation.

As a private lender, I have reduced interest rates and lowered payments for borrowers who owed me but could not afford to make payments. My borrowers have been able to hold on to property and survive to eventually make a profit. I made less of a profit, but by helping them survive we both came out better.

LONGER REPAYMENT TERMS (WITHOUT PREPAYMENT PENALTIES) ARE ALWAYS BETTER

If you like to pay off debt, as I do, then a short-term loan with large principal payments has some appeal. I have one loan that pays down just over $400 a month. If I break even on that property, I still make $400 a month—but when?

When do I benefit from that $400-a-month principal reduction? The answer: when I sell. Because I have the obligation to make the same loan payment next month, I get no advantage from the $400 paydown. I won't get it back until I sell.

My lender, on the other hand, gets the extra $400 each month. It makes their loan safer. It gives them a higher return on their money. That brings up the question: If it's good for the lender, is it bad for the borrower?

If I plan to keep this house for a long time or forever, does it make sense to pay down $400 a month, or would I be better off with the $400 a month in my pocket today? Your choice: $400 a month more cash flow or $400 a month saved up for you until you sell the house.

Hopefully, you voted for more cash in your pocket today. How can you have less principal paydown? Borrow with long-term loans from institutions and interest-only loans from investors and sellers whenever possible.

Every deal is a little different. If a seller insists on some amortization and the rest of the deal is good, take it. Most investors are good at math and if they lend you $100,000, they would rather keep their entire $100,000 invested with you and receive interest on the entire amount each month. Getting a little principal back each month that will go into a low-interest account is not wise investing.

Risk tolerance decreases with age. By learning to use safe leverage, you can continue to borrow wisely at every age. Although your personal holding period has limits, it's okay to get a new forty-year loan when you are eighty, as long as it's a safe loan with no personal guarantees, and the payments are ones that the tenants can easily repay.

Your heirs will probably inherit some real estate. If it is encumbered with safe debt, they can inherit more (two houses with 50 percent loans rather than one free-and-clear house). As I discussed earlier, this portfolio could have more cash flow.

NEVER SIGN A SHORT-TERM LOAN WITHOUT A WAY OUT

If you have bought property with owner financing, you have probably been asked to pay the loan off in a shorter time than you planned. It's not uncommon for sellers to ask for a "balloon clause" requiring that the note be paid in full at a certain date. This is dangerous for you as a buyer, since you cannot predict what the credit market will be like in, for example, five years.

It is reasonable and wise for you as a buyer to counter with this offer: "If you are unable to refinance the property in five years at a rate equal to or lower than the rate you have agreed to pay, you have the right to begin amortizing the loan for the next five years with payments based on the same interest rate and a thirty-year amortization schedule."

Ten years is generally long enough for the credit market to cycle. If you can't get a loan in five years, you may not be able to sell at a fair price, either. Building in an extension of time makes the financing safer.

8

BORROWING WITHOUT GOING TO A BANK

When I started investing in houses, I was a self-employed real estate salesman with no steady income. Not one banker in my town would loan me money to buy property. As it turned out, that was a key to my success. It forced me to learn how to buy property without going to a bank to borrow money.

Many real estate investors who are millionaires today, started with only a little money. Some did not have a job with a W-2, or great credit. They bought their first property with a small down payment, and then they bought another property as soon as they could. They continued to buy, one property at a time, negotiating better terms and prices as they learned more.

The secret to being able to buy property that will make you large profits is to learn how to borrow on terms that your tenants can repay with their monthly rent. Buying a property with little or nothing down is a great strategy, as long as you can afford to make the payments. If you can't afford to make the payments, you will never collect any profits.

Banks require investors who want to borrow to make a down payment, often 20 percent, and require good credit. They will only loan 80 percent of the purchase price or appraisal, whichever is lower. If you buy a house worth $200,000 for $150,000, they will only loan you 80 percent of the $150,000.

When you find a bargain, it is often because the sellers need to sell right away. If they could wait ninety days, they would and probably sell for more.

Unfortunately, banks will not make you a new loan in a few days. Borrowing from a bank takes longer and costs more than other sources. When you borrow from a bank you will pay high closing costs and they will charge you the current retail rate of interest. The paperwork you are required to sign will protect the bank, and if you read the fine print, you give them the right to take other assets that you own if you cannot repay the debt.

If you have a good job and good credit, banks will loan you money for a few house purchases. If you buy a lot of houses, you will find that lenders often have limits to the amount and number of loans that they will make you, and, eventually, the banks may refuse to make you more loans.

BORROWING A MILLION DOLLARS AND STILL SLEEPING WELL

How would you feel about owing a million dollars? If you buy more than five $200,000 houses, you could easily owe a million dollars. The key to sleeping well while you are in debt is knowing that you can repay the debt. When you buy rental houses, your tenants will repay your debt if you buy and finance wisely.

My friend Jack Miller said that the surest way to become a millionaire with real estate is to borrow a million dollars secured by property, and then pay it off. Even if the property is never appreciated, you would have your million dollars.

Jack is right. If you can learn how to borrow that million dollars safely so you can sleep well, then you are on your way to unlimited financial success. The safety comes from borrowing against property that generates enough income to repay the loan.

Most people can't conceive the idea of borrowing that much money, because they are thinking about going to the bank and qualifying for a million-dollar loan. You can borrow from sources other than banks without qualifying for a loan based on your income and credit.

Bankers have a lot of rules to follow. The rules are both imposed by the government and self-imposed by the banking industry. Before a banker lends you money on real estate, he will want an appraisal, a credit report, proof of your income, and a list of your other debts and assets. If you start buying property aggressively, you will soon reach the point where the rules will limit the number of loans you can have with one lender. These rules make borrowing from banks both time consuming and agonizing.

THINGS YOUR BANKER WON'T DO

1. Your banker won't make a decision fast enough to loan you the money to buy a really good deal.

A good deal is when a seller has *decided to sell today* (or in the next few days) and selling quickly is more important than the price. Often the seller is out of time and needs money today (or very soon) or something bad is going to happen.

I have purchased several homes from sellers a day or two before their house would be sold at a foreclosure auction. Although they may have had chances to sell before, they waited until the last minute to make a decision. At that point, there were few buyers willing to take the risk of buying on such short notice and able to close in one day.

Even though I have great credit and can qualify for a loan, there is not a banker in my town who can close a real estate loan the same day I call him. A home equity loan or line of credit could be used for quick purchases at bargain prices. However, these loans have variable interest rates and some are short-term loans. These terms make them dangerous loans for a long-term investor.

New federal consumer protection regulations (SAFE Act and Dodd-Frank Act) lengthen the time it takes a homeowner to get a bank loan and to close a real estate purchase. Some sellers just can't wait that long. Look for sellers who can't wait, and make them offers that allow them to finance either part of or all of the purchase price.

2. Your banker won't loan you more than 80 percent of the purchase price of an investment property.

If you wait to buy a house until you save up a 20 percent down payment, it may take you years to buy your first house. And, by then, houses will probably be more expensive, so waiting can cost you a lot.

If your goal is to buy a property with a smaller down payment, then you will have to find a lender other than a bank. Some sellers will sell you a property and finance most of or all of the price. Often they are sick—either sick of managing or sick of making payments. Look for burned-out investors who have bought several properties but never learned to manage. They will often sell to you with a low down payment and carry all the financing to get out of management. Even a small payment is more money than they can get when they rent to a tenant.

Some investors try to trick bankers into lending to them by using fake contracts or phony appraisals. This is called *bank fraud*, and you will go to jail if you get caught. Typically, the lender does not go to jail, just the borrower who provided false statements.

Beware of those who tell you to lie or use devious methods to buy or borrow. Understand that many lenders work on commission and that they are under pressure to lend money. If you are uncomfortable with what they are asking you to do, get a second opinion from another lender or an attorney.

3. Your banker won't make you a loan when prices are at their lowest.

When real estate prices are going up, it's typically easier to get a loan and bankers will make loans to investors. But when a recession comes and prices fall, banks stop making investor loans. You want to be able to buy when there is a recession. The prices are at their lowest during a down cycle.

4. Your banker won't make you a loan without regular monthly payments or with the first payment due several months from now.

In fact, bankers typically insist on monthly payments starting right away. This is a problem if you are buying a house that will sit empty for a while.

Sellers will often accept financing with more flexible terms and lower payments in the beginning that would allow you to have cash flow immediately. I have negotiated payments with seller financing starting in six months or longer after the closing date.

5. A banker won't loan money to someone who really needs it.

If you need it, then you must be in trouble or almost in trouble, and bankers hate trouble.

If you know you are going to need money one day, borrow before you need it. You may really need it because you are about to be temporarily unemployed, or divorced, or unable to pay your taxes. Whatever the reason, it will be hard to borrow once you are in trouble.

WHY A SELLER WILL DO WHAT YOUR BANKER WON'T DO

When a banker loans you money, he writes you a check. He is going to be very cautious and charge you a high rate of interest, because he has borrowed the money he is lending to you from his depositors. He has to pay them back, so he can't take big chances with their money.

When you buy a house from a seller who wants to get rid of it, the seller is not lending you money, he is waiting for his equity or profit from his house. This may be equity or profit that he will not get if he does not sell to you.

A seller is not as cautious as the banker when it comes to lending money. He just needs to be comfortable that you will make his payments and eventually pay him.

Consider the following actual purchase:

Selling price:	$200,000
Market value:	$225,000 to $250,000
Seller's purchase price twenty years earlier:	$60,000
Potential bank loan (80 percent of purchase price):	$160,000
Actual seller financing:	$180,000 payable over twenty years at 4 percent

With this house, the seller had a large profit because he or she had owned the house for twenty years. When a seller has a large profit or large equity, he is often willing to finance the purchase and receive payments and his profit over several years.

With $20,000 down, the seller has received one-third of what he paid for the property as a down payment. In addition, over the next twenty years he will receive payments totaling $261,782 (240 payments of $1,090.76). Compared to what he originally paid, the seller has made a great investment.

A banker making a $160,000 loan has no profit until you begin making payments. What looks like a risky deal to a banker with a $40,000 down payment can look very safe to the seller of a property.

BORROWING ON TERMS THAT YOUR TENANTS CAN AFFORD TO REPAY

A wonderful feature of investing in property is that you can structure the financing on a property so that your tenants make all the payments. When you borrow on terms that have payments that your tenants can afford to make, they will buy the house for you.

Sometimes this requires a combination of financing. For example, suppose that you can buy a house worth $200,000 to $220,000 for $180,000. The gross rents are $1,600 a month, and the net income after taxes, insurance, and repairs is about $1,000 a month.

If you borrowed the entire $180,000, what interest rate and term would you need to have payments low enough that your tenants would repay the loan?

To answer this question, you need either an amortization schedule or a financial calculator. You can get a financial calculator app on your phone if you don't want to buy the calculator. Learn how to calculate both payments for different loan amounts, terms and interest rates, and the rate of return on your investment. Then you will be able to compare two potential investments.

With a financial calculator, you can solve for one variable if you know the other three. With the preceding question in mind, what interest rate can I pay and how much time would it take to repay the $180,000 purchase price with $1,000 a month in net income?

I know the amount ($180,000) and the payment ($1,000). To find an answer to the interest rate or term, I need to plug in one of the variables. In this case, that is the loan term of thirty years.

Amount of Loan	Interest Rate	Term	Payment
$180,000	?	30 years	$1,000
		(360 months)	

The solution is 5.3%.

Borrowing Without Going to a Bank

Now suppose that you have to pay 7 percent today for the money you need to borrow. You could solve for the term you would need. If you know that you can borrow at 7 percent for thirty years, then you could solve for how much you can borrow:

Amount of Loan	Interest Rate	Term	Payment
?	7%	360	$1,000

The result is $150,307.

What if you cannot borrow enough money at today's rate to buy the house and repay it with the cash flow the tenants will produce? Then you need to borrow part of the purchase price at a lower rate, with lower payments or with deferred payments.

Suppose that you need to borrow a total of $180,000, and you find a source that will lend you $150,000 at 6 percent for thirty years. A smaller loan will have a lower interest rate.

Amount of Loan	Interest Rate	Term	Payment
$150,000	6%	360	$899

After making the $899 payment, you have $102.05 a month (this year, because your rent should increase with time) to use to pay the other $30,000. Each year your cash flow should increase as rents increase.

Here are four ways to repay $30,000 with $100 a month:

1. Pay the seller (or a friendly lender such as your parents) $100 a month without interest, with payments to increase as you raise the rent.
2. Pay the seller $100 a month beginning when you can raise the rent enough to start making that payment.
3. Pay the seller $100 a month now and agree to increase it as you increase the rents. You can take your best guess at rent increases and design a repayment schedule based on your projections: say, $100 a month for the first five years, $125 a month for the subsequent five years, and then $150 a month until it is paid in full.
4. Pay the seller the whole amount ($30,000) in one lump sum ten years from now. This may cause you to either refinance or sell at that time unless you have saved the money to make the payment.

BUYING EMPTY HOUSES WITH ZERO-INTEREST, SINGLE-PAYMENT NOTES

Owners with an empty house will finance the amount of their equity with no payments for a while if you begin making the payments on their existing bank loan instead. These sellers have a big problem; they own an empty house that may cost them $1,000 or more every month. Few people have an extra $1,000 a month in their budget that they can use to make payments on an empty house.

I have purchased many houses by agreeing to start making payments on an existing loan and agreeing to pay the sellers the amount of their equity, without payments or interest, when I sold their house. This could take years, but in the meantime, they don't have anymore big payments to make.

You may be asking how you will be able to make the big payments that the seller can't make. The answer is that you will rent the house to a tenant who will pay you enough to make the payments. Before you make an offer on any property, know how much it will rent for and what your operating expenses will be so that you know how large of a payment you can make.

Suppose that a seller owns this house:

Today's market value:	$200,000 to $250,000
Their existing loan:	$150,000
Your offer:	$50,000 when you resell the house

Offer the seller a note for $50,000 with no interest and no payments until you sell the house. You can agree if the house does not sell in ten years you will pay the note. You agree to begin making the payment on the existing $150,000 loan. Secure the $50,000 note with a second-position mortgage or deed of trust on the house. In the event that you cannot make the payments, you can deed the house back to the seller.

The major benefit for the seller is that he or she gets immediate relief from both the payments and the responsibility of maintaining the house. If the seller wants to buy another house, he or she can show the new lender the agreement with you in which you took responsibility for making the payments on the first loan.

You get to buy a house with nothing down that will produce enough income when rented to make the payments on the first loan. When the house appreciates enough that you can refinance it or sell it at an acceptable profit, you will have the cash to pay off the second loan to the seller.

SHORT-TERM BANK LOANS FOR EMERGENCIES

A line of credit is an unsecured bank loan that you can obtain based on your credit and ability to repay it. You borrow only what you need when you need it and typically pay interest only on the balance until you repay the loan. These interest-only payments are lower than payments required on an amortizing loan.

The disadvantage in having lines of credit is that there may be a requirement to pay off the loan within a short period of time. Another disadvantage is that the interest rate typically is tied to the *prime rate*, or the rate set by the big banks. This rate can change with time, and your payments can increase.

A home equity line of credit (often called a HELOC) is a loan that is secured by your personal home. Some lenders will allow HELOCs on investment houses. Because it is secured, there is less risk to the lender, and the interest rate is often lower than you can negotiate on an unsecured line of credit. Again, you can typically arrange to pay interest on the outstanding balance only, although the interest rate will change with time.

These loans are useful for buying a house that you plan on selling for a short-term profit or selling to an investor to recover your investment and keeping half interest. They are not advisable for a house you want to hold for many years, because the rates and your payments could increase dramatically.

If you borrow using your home equity line at 5 percent and rates jump, you could soon be paying 10 percent interest, or twice your original payment. If you borrowed to buy a house and the rent just covered your payments, then with a higher interest rate, the rents would not cover the payments.

If you cannot repay a home equity loan, you could lose your home.

Use this money carefully. Only use it for emergencies, like an unexpected roof replacement or to buy a house that you know you can sell for a short-term profit. Know that when interest rates are rising rapidly, it may be harder to sell a property quickly for a profit.

WHY YOU SHOULD NOT REFINANCE ONE HOUSE TO BUY ANOTHER

If you are committed to buying several houses, your strategy for buying and financing them is important to your long-term success. Simply buying houses won't make you rich.

New investors often assume that the best way to get the down payment for a second house is to refinance the first house. Logically, they would then refinance the second house for the down payment on the third house and continue to refinance to pull out cash for new investments.

Refinancing can be a good strategy to reduce your interest costs when rates drop. If you can borrow at a lower rate and for a longer term, your payments will drop and your cash flow will increase.

When you refinance and pull cash out of a property, you are increasing your debt, and if your payments increase, you are increasing your risk of losing that property. Consider the result of refinancing a house appraised at $180,000 to get the down payment to buy another one:

Appraised value of house:	$180,000
Percentage a bank will loan to investor:	80 percent
Amount of new loan:	$144,000
Estimated closing costs (3 percent):	$4,320
Payoff on old loan:	$100,000
Net cash available for down payments:	$39,680

REFINANCING DOES NOT MAKE YOU RICHER

Note that before you refinanced the house in this example you had $80,000 in equity, the difference between the value of the property and the loan balance. After you refinance, you would have $36,000 in equity and $39,680 in cash for a total of $75,680. Your net worth has dropped by the amount of the refinancing cost.

Refinancing is not a profitable move unless you reduce your interest cost significantly so that the interest you save repays your cost of refinancing in five years or less. If you sell the house in less than five years, you will not even recover your refinancing costs. Lenders know that many loans are either paid off or refinanced in five years or less, so refinancing is a profitable business for them.

Temptation is another risk of refinancing. Despite your intentions to buy another investment property with the proceeds, those new cars and exotic vacations are very tempting. Either have the house you want to buy under contract so that you know where you will spend the refinancing proceeds, or put the funds in a separate account (not your personal checking account). If the money is in your personal account, you may yield to temptation and spend some or all of it on toys or good times.

An alternative strategy may be to put a second mortgage on this investment house and avoid paying the closing costs on the $100,000 balance on the old loan that you get no benefit from paying off. Second mortgages often have higher interest rates. Compare the increased interest cost to the closing costs you can save by not refinancing the whole amount.

Closing costs, when borrowing, typically include a credit report, an appraisal, title insurance on the new loan, recording fees, state taxes, some-times points (interest paid in advance), and miscellaneous fees that the lender tacks on. These costs often equal about 3 percent of the new loan amount.

Whenever you borrow, recognize that some of these costs are the same regardless of how much you borrow. If you only borrowed $124,000 in the preceding example, netting you $20,000, but had to pay closing costs on the whole amount, your costs would be a much higher percentage of the money you borrowed (4,320/20,000 = 21.6%; 4,320/39,680 = 10.88%).

REFINANCING INCREASES YOUR RISK

Suppose that you owned a house today that is worth $200,000 with a $100,000, 6 percent loan with a payment of $700 and a net rent (after all operating expenses, maintenance, taxes, and insurance) of $900. You would have $200 cash flow each month. If you refinance to an 80 percent loan, you could raise $60,000, less your closing costs, and if the interest rate and the term stayed the same, your payment would be $1,146. Your cash flow on this house would change from a plus $200 to a negative $246.

Before refinancing:

House value:	$200,000
Loan:	$100,000
Cash flow:	+$200 per month

Result: The risk of loss to foreclosure is very low.

After refinancing:

Loan: $160,000
Cash flow: $246
Result: The risk of loss to foreclosure is high.

By refinancing, you put your remaining equity of $40,000 at a higher risk of loss.

Before you refinanced this house it was a safe investment; you had $200 a month in cash flow. If there was a recession in your town, you could lower your rent by $200 a month and still make the payments. After you refinance you have a $246 loss each month, and if you can't make up the difference you could lose the house to foreclosure.

If you take the money you borrowed and bought two more houses, you could buy other $200,000 houses, hopefully for no more than $180,000. With your $30,000 down payment on each house you would owe $150,000. At 6 percent and on a thirty-year term, the payment would be $900 a month. Each house would break even. Your total portfolio of three houses would be a loss of $246 a month.

A BETTER STRATEGY

Rather than refinancing a loan, consider the difference in your risk if you used the cash flow from your first investment property to acquire another house. Suppose you find a house with an existing loan on it that will rent for $200 a month less than the loan payments. It might look like this:

Market value:	$200,000 to $220,000
Loan balance:	$180,000, payable over thirty years at 6 percent interest at $1,080 a month
Your net rent on the house would be the same:	$900
The monthly cash flow on the house:	−$180

Borrowing Without Going to a Bank

The positive cash flow on the house you already own could be used to make up the difference each month. As a side note, the principal paydown on this loan would be about $180 a month. Even though it requires an additional investment of $180 a month, the loan is being reduced each month by about the same amount.

Consider the difference between refinancing and using the cash flow from your existing house to buy another house. You have not refinanced your first house, so it still has a safe loan. If you had to reduce your rent, you could still afford the payment on that house so you would not lose your equity.

Say you have bought a new house by taking over existing financing or by giving a seller a note payable at $1,080 a month. Because you did not borrow this money from a bank, or hard money lender, there would be no personal guarantee. If you could not make the payments, you could lose this house, but you would not be putting your first house at risk.

9

ATTRACTING AND USING INVESTOR MONEY TO INCREASE YOUR PROFITS

There are many passive investors who have their cash in a low-yielding bank account or who are unhappy with their returns in the stock market. Others may now own investment real estate but want to retire from active management.

They are looking for an alternate and safe investment with a reasonable return. They have no interest in doing the work it takes to buy and manage a property but could be interested in investing with someone who would do all of the work.

If you have the knowledge and ability to buy and manage a house that will produce a profit but are short on cash to buy property, then investing with others can benefit you both. You can buy property that you could not buy without an investor. The investor can participate in the profits that the property produces and earn a better return.

IDENTIFYING POTENTIAL INVESTORS

Suppose that you find a great buy and need money for a down payment. Make a list of people who you know who like real estate and believe that it is a good investment. They do not invest in real estate because they don't want to deal with the tenants, nor do they want to negotiate the purchase and sale of a house. They don't know how to make a good buy or manage tenants, and they won't take the time to learn—but they are great prospects as passive investors.

There are four traits important in any potential investor:

- Honesty
- Intelligence
- A long-term outlook
- Enough money or credit to acquire a house

> *Never get involved with someone who has*
> *to borrow the money to invest.*

Consider whom you now know who has these traits and who may want to invest with you. They may be any of the following:

- Business associates—employer, employees, landlord
- People to whom you now owe money
- Family members who need a better return on their money
- Other investors who buy in your town

You may also want to consider those who know your business and may be able to refer others, such as . . .

- Your accountant
- Your attorney
- Your insurance agent
- A title company that you do business with
- A Realtor you do business with
- Contractors who do work for you

DON'T JUST ASK THEM IF THEY WOULD LIKE TO INVEST

Instead, you should find a house that you would like to buy and make an offer on it "subject to" arranging financing that is acceptable to you. After this is decided, you should talk to potential investors, show them your contract and the house. If they are interested, ask them if they would like to invest with you in this house if you agreed to take care of the management. Show them the estimated loan payments, gross rents, and expected expenses so that they understand how you will repay any money borrowed and how much cash flow the house will potentially produce.

If this is not a deal that they want today, ask if they know anyone who might be interested. Your time has not been wasted if they say no. They may be a potential investor for another deal in the future, and they may tell their friends about you.

Do not ask others to invest with you until you can buy at good prices and know how to manage. You build credibility with potential investors when you can talk about other property that you own and manage now.

ADVANTAGES TO USING AN INVESTOR'S CASH FOR THE DOWN PAYMENT

1. It does not have to be repaid until you sell the property.
2. You make no payments on it and pay no interest until you sell the property.
3. By using an investor's cash to make a larger down payment and close quickly, you can negotiate a bigger discount on the price.
4. Using the investor's cash for a larger down payment will reduce the debt on the property and increase the cash flow, making the house a safer investment.

As you start to invest, a source of money for down payments can allow you to buy property with less debt that will have more cash flow. If you buy a house with a low down payment and finance most of the purchase price, most if not all of your cash flow will go toward repaying the debt. If you borrow too much or borrow on bad terms, you may have to make an additional investment each month to pay the loan.

When an investor makes a larger down payment on the house, then the debt will be less, and the payments should be lower. This allows you to buy and have immediate cash flow.

The example below shows a comparison between buying a house with high leverage by yourself and using an investor's money for the down payment. This house had a fair market value of between $170,000 and $180,000.

Plan A: Buy the house by yourself with an 80 percent loan

House purchase price:	$150,000
Down payment:	$30,000
Net rent (after all expenses):	$800
Loan payment ($120,000, thirty-year, 6 percent):	$720
Monthly cash flow:	+$80

Plan B: Buy the house with an investor making the down payment

House purchase price:	$150,000
Down payment:	$50,000
Net rent (after all expenses):	$800
Loan payment (thirty-year, 6 percent):	$477
Monthly cash flow:	+$323

Notice a couple of things. The larger down payments allow the borrower to get a better interest rate. If you could qualify for the lower rate yourself and you had the $30,000 down payment, I would advise you to buy this house by yourself.

Splitting Profits Fairly

With any joint venture, it is important to agree up front on how you will split profits. Many joint ventures pay the organizer and the manager of the investment both a commission and a share of the profits before the investor gets his money back or any share of the profit.

This seems unfair to the investor, who is taking most of the risk. A fairer approach is to split profits 50/50 with an investor, each participating in the cash flow, both positive and negative, and then returning the investor's initial investment before splitting the profits on the sale 50/50.

This gives the buyer/manager the incentive to buy a property with profit potential and then manage it well, since he only gets paid as the property produces a profit.

If the investor participates in 50 percent of the cash flow and appreciation, each would receive half of the $323 a month and half of the eventual profit on the sale. You, as the manager, would have monthly cash flow and own half of a house with equity that will grow over time.

Although the cash flow is low in the first few years, it will increase with time and, in addition, the loan is being paid down each month and the property may appreciate with time. Never make a guarantee of profits. Show the actual numbers today, and then plan on holding a property until it doubles in value.

BOTH YOU AND THE INVESTOR SHARE TAX BENEFITS

Profit produced by buying the property below the market will be taxed at the lower capital gains rate. You and the investor also may be able to shelter some of your current income from taxes with the depreciation the house produces.

You will agree to find and buy the property, manage the property, and then—years from now—handle the sale. The investor's part is to put up the down payment and, if necessary, qualify for and sign the loan. When you borrow using an investor, limit your loan to a maximum of 75 percent of the value of the house, and borrow for the longest term possible so that your rents will cover the payments. It will be a low-risk loan and should be an easy loan for any investor with good credit to obtain.

Your plan is to hold the house until it doubles in value, and then sell and split the profits with the investor 50/50, after repaying the down payment he made.

Today's market value:	$200,000 to $225,000
The purchase price:	$175,000
New loan:	$125,000
Down payment from investor:	$50,000

You hold the house until it doubles in value.

Sales price when it doubles:	$400,000
Approximate loan balance:	$100,000 (this amount will vary with time)
Gross sales proceeds:	$300,000
Repay the down payment:	$50,000
Balance of sales proceeds:	$250,000
Your 50 percent of profit:	$125,000
Investor's 50 percent of profit:	$125,000

You made $125,000 plus half of the cash flow with no money invested, but you used your time and skill to find a good deal, buy it, and manage the property and the tenants. The investor made $125,000 plus half of the cash flow in profit on his $50,000 investment, without ever talking to a seller, tenant, or a buyer.

Finding a bargain, negotiating a below-market price and maybe great terms, managing the property well until it doubles in value, and then selling it for a retail price is worth a lot. Sharing half the profits when one party puts up the money and the other provides the brains *is not fair*. It's a great deal for the investor. Do a good job finding and managing deals and you will have many people wanting to invest with you.

How much would an investor earn on $50,000 in a year where it is invested now, say, in a mutual fund or savings account? How much would they have in ten years? Compare that number with the return they would make owning half a house with you.

PROTECTING YOURSELF AND THE INVESTOR

There are several ways to hold title to a house with an investor. You want to protect both parties' interests and use easy-to-understand documents and agreements.

A simple way to protect your interest is to be named on the title to the property. Document your agreement to manage the property with a short and clear management agreement. Because you are also an owner of the property, you would not need a real estate license to manage the property (a nonowner may need a license to manage investment real estate in some states).

HOLDING TITLE AS TENANTS IN COMMON

A simple way for you and investors to own a house together is to have the investor buy the house, finance it, and then deed to you an undivided one-half interest with the loan in place. All these papers can be signed at one meeting at the closing of the property and be recorded in the proper order in the public records. You then would be an undivided one-half owner on the public records, holding title as tenants in common.

This is not a partnership, and *you should not call it a partnership*, nor file a partnership tax return. Each owner actually owns an undivided half of the house. Each owns half the roof, half the lot, and so on.

Because you actually own one-half of a house, you could sell your half interest to another person, but few buyers are interested in buying half a house. The plan is to hold the whole house until you sell both halves to a new owner.

If something unexpected happens to your investor—he dies, loses a lawsuit, or files bankruptcy—then his half may be transferred to a new owner, but you would still own your half. An advantage of holding title as tenants in common is that claims against the investor's half will not attach to the other half that you own.

All that is required to hold title as tenants in common is the proper language in the deed. You can go into title and borrow the money together to acquire the house. Or, as suggested earlier, the investor can go into title, borrow the money, and then deed one-half interest to you. If you buy and borrow together, then you will have to furnish financial statements and pay for credit reports and other expenses.

HOLDING TITLE IN A TRUST, CORPORATION, OR LLC

Another way to hold title that has the advantage of keeping the names of the owners off the public records is to form a trust, corporation, or limited-liability company (LLC) or limited-liability partnership (LLP) to own the property. These entities either can pass through the income and expenses to the owners or pay the taxes before making distributions. An advantage of using an entity that can be taxed as a partnership is that you can make disproportionate distributions of income and allocations of expenses.

These entities require documentation and you may be required to file an annual tax return. To be used wisely, they require a good understanding of how they work.

One disadvantage is that lenders often will not lend money on properties that are owned by trusts or other entities. The bankers may require you to hold the title personally to finance or refinance. Some states require you to use an attorney to evict tenants owned by corporations or LLCs. Insuring properties held in different entities may be a challenge. If using these entities to hold title sounds more complicated and expensive, it is.

When you are dealing with other people's money, you want to be cautious, and you want to be sure that documents are prepared, executed, and recorded or filed properly. If you want to form a separate entity to hold title, find a competent attorney with lots of experience in forming these entities. There are advantages and disadvantages to taking title in a separate entity. Obtain both legal and tax advice before spending thousands of dollars to form and maintain an entity that you may not need.

MY FIRST INVESTOR AND THE DEALS THAT WE MADE

My first investor was Fred, a retired attorney with a good income and great credit. He understood real estate but had no interest in being an active investor with any management responsibilities.

I would find houses that he could buy at a bargain price, and then Fred would make the necessary down payment to get a low-interest-rate, long-term loan. Fred would close on the house in his name alone and acquire the new loan.

He then would deed me one-half interest in the house and we would own the house as tenants in common. I gave him my personal note (I.O.U.) for an amount equal to one-half of his down payment.

When we sold a property, we would split the proceeds and I would repay my note to him, which had no interest and required no payments, to repay my half of the down payment.

Today's market value:	$200,000 to $225,000
Purchase price:	$175,000
New loan:	$125,000
Fred's down payment:	$50,000

We hold the house until it doubles in value.

Sales price when it doubles:	$400,000
Approximate loan balance:	$100,000 (this amount will vary with time)
Gross sale proceeds:	$300,000
Fred's 50 percent:	$150,000
My 50 percent:	$150,000
My note due to Fred:	$25,000
My net cash:	$125,000

Fred has traded the interest he could collect on the $25,000 he loaned me to buy my half interest in the house for the profit he earned. We shared the cash flow the house produced while we owned it.

His return was greater than he could achieve with other investments and had less downside risk. Fred's cash flow and long-term profit totaled more than 10 percent a year.

My profit of $125,000 was a great return, since I borrowed my share of the down payment from Fred. The proof that it was good for both of us is that we did it over and over again.

BORROWING FROM OTHER INVESTORS

If you find an investor like Fred and make him money, he may be a source of financing to you for properties that you do not own together. Suppose that you found a house that you could buy from an owner who would finance most of the purchase price for you.

For example:

Today's market value:	$200,000 to $225,000
Purchase price:	$175,000
Owner financing:	$150,000
Down payment needed:	$25,000

Your "Fred" would have confidence in your abilities and trust you after you have owned property together for a few years. He should be willing to lend you the $25,000 that you need to buy this house and take a note secured by the house at a reasonable interest rate.

BORROWING ON INTEREST-ONLY TERMS

When you borrow from an investor like Fred, the investor prefers to keep her capital invested. She doesn't want you to amortize a loan, that is, pay back a little of the principal each month. She would prefer that you pay interest on the entire amount as long as you need her money.

When an investor sees that she can collect significantly more interest than the bank will pay her with an acceptable amount of risk, she will want to invest more with you.

Many people have money in self-directed retirement accounts or other accounts that they will need in the short run and are not willing to invest in property. They may be willing to invest in a relatively short-term (five to ten years) loan that would pay them more interest than they could earn in their bank account.

Bankers have high overhead and pay depositors a small fraction of what they charge their borrowers. If you cut out the middleman, the bank, you can borrow directly from depositors and pay them far more than the bank will. Investors can still be an affordable source of funds for you.

An additional advantage of borrowing from a private source is that you sometimes can negotiate a loan with no payments due until you sell the property. If your lender is a pension plan that is not going to distribute the income to the beneficiaries for ten more years, the fund doesn't need the money back soon. The fund can make you a three-year loan with no payments for three years with interest to accrue that you could use to buy a property and repay it with interest when you sell.

The biggest concern of private lenders is getting their money back. They are not as concerned about earning a high rate of interest as they are in getting their money back. Oversecure any money that you borrow from a private lender. Give private lenders more than one property if you need to so that they will feel secure. A secure lender is a happy lender, who sleeps well, and such a lender will lend to you at a reasonable rate of interest.

Avoid lenders who charge high interest. Only a speculator who is buying and selling a property in a short time can afford these rates. The speculator is giving the lender a share of the profit and has to pay the high rate, because he is often borrowing near 100 percent of the purchase price. Buying and selling is much higher risk than buying and renting.

RULES FOR INVESTING WITH OTHERS

- Don't buy properties that you don't know how to manage.
- Do buy at a price and on terms that will produce cash flow.
- Don't make projections.
- Never invest with someone who has to borrow the money to invest.
- Don't overpromise.
- Do write down your agreement in such a way that it cannot be misunderstood in years to come.

- Protect your interest by taking title to half interest in the property to secure your interest.
- Protect the investor's interest by having him on title for half interest, plus give the investor a note secured by your interest in the property to secure his cash invested.
- Account for and distribute income annually, and keep a cash reserve for unforeseen expenses.

Who You Invest with Is Important

- If the property needs financing, the investor should have great credit in order to get a low-interest-rate loan.
- Choose carefully: whom you do business with is more important than the deal.
- When a deal is too one-sided, it will go bad.
- Look for investors who can do more than one deal—who have what you need, lots of credit or lots of money
- Make every deal good for your investor and she will want to do another with you and she will tell her friends.
- Structure deals to give both parties what they need.

10

USING A REAL ESTATE CONTRACT TO YOUR ADVANTAGE

"Those who don't read have no advantage over those who can't."

—Mark Twain

Contracts to purchase real estate have evolved over the years, but one thing has not: few actually read the contracts they sign. When you are about to invest thousands of dollars and promise to pay much more, take the time to read a contract word for word before you sign it. Once you have read a few, you will recognize most of the standard clauses, terms, and conditions. More important, you will be able to identify and negotiate the parts of the contract that are most relevant to you.

Do you need a written contract to buy, sell, or lease real estate? You can answer no and be correct, but there is a catch. You do need a written contract if you ever want to enforce it in a courtroom. The statute of frauds requires that a contract regarding interest in real estate must be in writing and signed by the parties involved in order to be enforceable.

Another important reason to have a written agreement is unless both parties agree and understand the agreement or have a "meeting of the minds," then the contract is not enforceable. A signed contract is evidence of this understanding.

A third reason to have a written agreement is to help everyone remember what they agreed to. All parties should understand the agreement the day they sign it, but that is no guarantee that they will remember it that way on the day of the closing. Relying on memories is a bad strategy in any business transaction. There is a good chance that the buyer and seller may remember things differently weeks, months, or years later. The written agreement is an essential memory aid.

A very practical reason to write down the important details is that the agent or attorney who will be closing the transaction will rely on the contract for the terms of the sale and of any financing involved. Another reason to have a clearly written agreement is to provide you with a way to get out of the contract if you decide not to buy (or sell). A way out is often called a loophole or contingency.

A written contract is also a checklist for items that are important for you to negotiate. The price, the down payment, the closing date, who will pay the expenses of closing, when you will close, and much more are all written into your purchase contract.

KEEPING IT SIMPLE

Real estate contracts can be confusing and even intimidating. Some agreements are dozens of pages long, and most have been prepared by attorneys and contain language that can be difficult to understand.

With preparation, you can understand any contract and use contracts to your advantage. The key is to take the time to read and understand any contract before you are under pressure to sign during a negotiation.

DON'T SIGN UNTIL YOU TAKE THE TIME TO READ IT

You may spend dozens of hours finding and researching a good deal, and if you buy it, you will spend hundreds of more hours managing and eventually selling it. Set aside the time you need to read any contract carefully before you sign it. Do this alone, without the pressure of others waiting on you to read it. You should never sign a document that you do not fully understand. You may discover later that you have made concessions worth thousands of dollars unknowingly because you signed a contract that you did not understand.

If you are presented with a contract that an attorney drafted, be cautious of any words or phrases that you do not understand. If an attorney prepared it, he or she was probably working for the other party, and the conditions in the contract may benefit the other party.

If you're using your attorney, get him or her to send you a copy a day before you intend to sign it so that you can take your time and read it carefully. Attorneys occasionally use confusing or unclear wording. Make them use words that you understand. One attorney once prepared a document for me that was so convoluted that he could not even explain it to me. He had cut and pasted several paragraphs from another document that even he did not understand. It was back to the drawing board for him, without pay.

FORM CONTRACTS PROTECT THE SELLER, REALTOR, AND ATTORNEY

Remember that a Realtor almost always represents the seller and that a committee of agents and attorneys typically designs these contracts. These form contracts are designed to legally bind both parties but often have clauses that give the seller, Realtor, and the attorney more protection than the buyer.

As a buyer, you need to understand what you are signing and carefully read any form contract that you receive ahead of time. Get a copy of a contract (a Realtor with whom you might do business would be a good source), and practice by filling in all the blanks as if you actually were purchasing a house. Read all of the fine print to see what it requires you to do and what happens if you do not perform.

Beware: There is no "standard" contract. Even these form contracts are often modified to give one party an advantage. It is important to use a contract that is designed for the type of transaction you are making. A contract designed for residential sales would have inspection and financing clauses that you would not find in a contract used to buy and sell land. A contract to buy a commercial building or mobile home park would be significantly different.

USING THE SELLER'S CONTRACT

When you are buying, sometimes the seller will have a contract on hand, and it can be to your advantage to use her contract. Using an agreement that the seller will prepare or fill out, is evidence that she understands the agreement. It would be unlikely that she could raise misunderstanding the agreement as a successful defense.

Read the seller's contract carefully and look for unusual provisions that favor the seller. Take your time, and, if possible, take a copy of the contract with you so that you can read it word for word before you sign it. If you are ready to make the offer immediately, go over the contract with the seller line by line, asking him questions about anything that is unclear to you.

USING AN INFORMAL AGREEMENT

Although you need to be careful in writing down your first few deals, professional buyers often use an informal agreement before actually filling out a binding contract. In Donald Trump's *The Art of the Deal*, he explains how he typically negotiates all the important parts of a deal with the seller without using a contract and then gives his notes to his attorneys to incorporate in a binding agreement. These are $100-million deals.

The only contract I had for one of the largest transactions I was involved in was a large brown envelope on which the seller and I diagrammed a deal including thirteen properties and several financing transactions. It closed without a hitch because we both wanted to close and were able to work out the details that we had overlooked using the envelope.

When I am buying a house, I will often outline my offer one step at a time on a yellow pad or blank sheet of paper so that the sellers can both hear me and see in simple terms how I am willing to buy their house. Most sellers have little experience in buying or selling property. You cannot go too slowly or make it too simple when explaining an offer.

Sellers have two big questions they want answered:

1. How much will I be paid?
2. When will I be paid?

FILLING IN THE BLANKS

Most contracts you use will have blanks to fill in or, if a lawyer is preparing the contract, questions that need to be answered. You should practice filling out a form contract with real numbers. Fill in every blank and think about which ones are most important to you. The more comfortable you are filling out a contract, the more comfortable you will be presenting an offer. If you are nervous and do not understand the contract, the seller (or buyer if you are selling) will be nervous too and may be too nervous to sign.

NAMING THE BUYER

When buying, list the buyer's name *and use the language "and/or assigns."* Now you have the right to assign the contract if you find another buyer who will pay more before the closing. If you list an entity as the buyer, sign the contract as the representative of that entity. For example, "John Schaub, President" or "John Schaub, Managing Member" or "John Schaub, Trustee."

THE AMOUNT OF EARNEST MONEY WITH THE CONTRACT

It is not in your best interest to make a large earnest money deposit. The only reason to make a large deposit is to convince the seller that you are a serious buyer. You can get the seller's attention with less money by making an offer that closes in a week.

Offer a small amount of money as earnest money. The Realtor may ask for 5 percent or more of the selling price. Some contracts will say that this money is retained by the agents as a commission, even if there is a default and it does not close. One hundred dollars is enough earnest money if your offer calls for a quick closing. If the agent has another buyer, they can submit their offer as a backup, so it does not hurt their chances of collecting a commission. It's an easy sell.

You may be able to get your deposit back, if you decide not to buy, depending on the conditions of the contract. However, it could take a while and it may be a hassle to get your deposit returned. If it's only $100 instead of $10,000, it's not as important to get it back so quickly.

THE TERMS AND CONDITIONS

ALL CASH. The simplest for the seller to understand. The cash is payable at the closing.

SUBJECT TO ACQUIRING A LOAN. This condition gives the buyer the opportunity to tie up the property while he looks for suitable financing. If the buyer cannot obtain financing that he likes, then he can cancel the agreement. Beware of clauses regarding financing that are too specific (a specific amount, loan term, or interest rate). Ask for as much time as possible.

CONTRACT TERMS WHEN THE SELLER AGREES TO FINANCE THE SALE. When the seller will agree to sell to you on terms acceptable to you both, include those details in your purchase contract.

CONDITION AND DELIVERY OF TITLE. To ensure that you acquire a good title, you will want to obtain a title search and title insurance policy. Both attorneys and title companies provide this service. Your contract should provide that you will receive title free and clear of all liens and encumbrances. Read your title insurance commitment carefully; it can list exceptions to a clear title and issue insurance that does not cover the exceptions. A common exception is unpaid property taxes, which will be prorated at the closing and the new buyer will be responsible for payment when they become due.

CLOSING DATE. A fast closing is often appealing to a seller who is in a hurry. The best buys are from sellers who have an almost immediate need for cash and are willing to sell at a bargain price to get it.

INSPECTION CLAUSE. Ideally, you want an inspection period that runs until the closing. If you are closing in a week or two, this should not be objectionable to the seller. You can make an offer to buy the property in "as is" condition, subject to an inspection. If you find defects that are too expensive to remedy, then you should be able to cancel the contract and receive a refund of your deposit. Of course, instead of canceling, you could renegotiate the contract to compensate you for the undisclosed defects.

The inspection clause could require the seller to fix items that cost up to a certain percentage of the purchase price. (If you're selling, set a low limit.) Buyers and their inspectors will always find something wrong with the property. There are no perfect houses.

When you are the seller, you want the buyer to approve the property within a short period of time *or* to provide you a list of the deficiencies in the property in writing. As the seller, you may want the right to fix the deficiencies and close the deal or the right to cancel the contract. If problems are found, the seller may want to give the buyer a certain amount of credit to expedite the closing of the deal.

Regardless of what the contact says, with mutual agreement you can negotiate a settlement when a problem is found. If you are selling, it is better to simply give the buyer a credit and to let him make the repairs. This gets the house closed faster and puts the burden of making the repair on the buyer. If the seller makes the repair, it is common for the buyer to complain about the quality of the repair work. Don't put yourself in this position.

When you are the buyer, you may want the seller to make the repairs, which gives you more time before you close. If you are borrowing money to buy the house, the lender may insist that the repairs are done before they will make a loan.

Just before closing (typically on the day of the closing, within hours of the time the papers are signed), the buyer inspects the house one more time. This is commonly called a *walk-through inspection*, and the purpose is to ensure that the house is in the condition promised in the contract and is vacant and empty.

Again, this inspection is better for the buyer than for the seller. If the seller has not made agreed-on repairs or has not left the house empty and clean, then the buyer has several choices. First, the buyer can refuse to close until the house is put in good condition. Second, he can insist on holding back part of the seller's proceeds until the house is clean and in good repair. Or third, he can renegotiate the price of the house.

Often, the seller just wants to get the deal closed and is willing to renegotiate the price. If this situation comes up when you are buying, be prepared to ask for a lower price that reflects the cost of the needed repairs or cleaning.

CLOSING COSTS

By custom, and sometimes by law, buyers pay certain closing costs and sellers pay certain closing costs. Sometimes a lender, such as the Veterans Administration (VA) or the Federal Housing Administration (FHA), will require that a seller pay the buyer's closing costs. Generally, with the exception of these government-insured or -funded loans you can negotiate who will pay these often substantial costs.

First, find out if your state requires a seller or buyer to pay a certain cost, for instance, the tax to record the deed or note. Next, determine which costs customarily are paid by the buyer and which costs are paid by the seller, such as title insurance, appraisals, loan closing fees, and so on. Although many of these fees are typically paid by the buyer, they still may be negotiable.

Just as a buyer can ask for a credit for repairs that need to be made, the buyer can also ask for a credit toward the closing costs of a new loan.

Paying a higher price and getting a credit for the closing costs may allow a buyer to borrow a higher percentage of the purchase price.

ASSUMING OR TAKING SUBJECT TO EXISTING LOANS AND LIENS

When you purchase a property that has an existing loan or existing liens recorded against it, you have three choices:

1. You can pay off those loans and liens.
2. You can assume the obligations and agree to pay them.
3. You can buy the house, paying the seller for his or her equity, and take title to the property *subject to* the loans or liens on the property.

If you agree to assume a loan, you are agreeing to become responsible for repaying the amount owed on the loan. If the lender is an institution, they will often require that you apply for a loan assumption and charge you for that privilege. There is often a fee, and when you assume the loan, it will show up on your credit report.

If there are liens to other creditors, you can agree to pay them off at closing or assume the responsibility to pay them. If you agree to pay them off, then the seller may hold you to that agreement, and if you do not pay them, the seller may sue you as a way to force you to pay the creditor. Be careful what you agree to when assuming a loan or a lien. Read the language in the contract carefully, and, if necessary, modify it to protect yourself.

When you take *subject to* rather than assuming a loan, you are not agreeing to pay these loans or liens; you are simply acknowledging that there is a loan or a lien against the property. Your contract should clearly state that you are buying subject to the loans, and the seller should understand what this means. The loan will still be in the seller's name.

Because the loan is in her name, it may affect the seller's ability to borrow money. If she is facing foreclosure, she is far better off if you begin making the payments rather than letting the loan go further into default. When you begin making on-time payments on the loan, it will actually improve her credit. Most sellers who will sell to you subject to a loan are in financial distress and cannot make their payments. The lender is also in better shape when you begin making payments. The lender normally would rather have the payments than the property.

Of course, if you buy a property and take title subject to a loan and then are unable to make the payments, you will lose your down payment and any other money you invest in the property. But—and this is an important but—you have no legal responsibility to pay such a loan. If you decide to walk away from this property because you cannot make a profit, you can walk away with a clear conscience.

Don't buy a property unless you are confident that you will make money from renting and/or selling it. In more than thirty years of buying properties and taking title subject to existing loans, I have made money on every deal, and in every case I made the payments.

One reason to take title subject to existing loans and liens is because the seller owes more on the property than you are willing to assume. You want to avoid the personal responsibility for repayment.

Some properties are burdened with high-risk debt, debt with a high interest rate, or a short-term loan that requires high payments. You do not want to guarantee to make payments on this high-risk debt. If you cannot make the payments, you want the option to give back the property to the seller or to the lender without any further responsibility.

In the last recession, several builders gave me the equity in their new houses, and I agreed to take them subject to their debt and began making payments to the lender. The builders were unable to make the payments and faced foreclosure and potential bankruptcy. While bankruptcy is more common now than in the past, many people are still proud of their good credit record. They will do all they can to avoid a foreclosure or a bankruptcy.

The lenders were delighted to begin receiving payments. I had to scramble to find good tenants during the recession, but they always appear when the rent is right.

THE RIGHT TO RENEGOTIATE OR DISCOUNT EXISTING LOANS AND LIENS

If you offer to buy a house subject to the existing loans and liens, you may be able to renegotiate the terms of these loans or negotiate a discount.

A young couple was trying to sell me their house, which had an existing loan with high payments. I agreed to buy the house, but only if they would allow me to negotiate with their lender to lower their payments. (They needed to be part of this process because the lender would not negotiate with me without their permission.)

The lender agreed to lower the payments by about $300 a month, I bought the house, and I was able to rent it for enough to make the payments.

Another seller had a bank loan and another loan to the builder that he had bought the house from, and a third lien on the house owed to an attorney for an unpaid legal bill. In talking with the seller, I learned that the builder had promised to make repairs and had never made them and that the attorney had not been successful in suing the builder.

I agreed to buy the house and take "subject to" the bank loan but not formally assume it. I further agreed to close subject to being able to negotiate both the builder's lien and the attorney's lien to my satisfaction. The seller then gave me permission to negotiate with both the builder and the attorney. I contacted both the builder and the attorney and offered to pay them that week if they would accept less money. Both agreed to a substantial discount and were happy to receive the money. I was able to buy the house at a significant discount because of the discount the lien holders agreed to take.

Today's market value:	$150,000 to $170,000
Bank loan:	$100,000 (taken subject to)
Builder loan:	$30,000 (paid off for $5,000)
Attorney lien:	$20,000 (paid off for $4,000)

SPECIFIC PERFORMANCE

A specific performance clause requires one party (or both parties) to fulfill the contract. It is more likely that the seller would be required to sell the property than a buyer would be forced to buy the house. But either or both parties can be held to the terms of the contract if there is a specific performance clause. When you are the buyer, you want to be able to walk away from a contract with the right to forfeit your deposit. Being able to walk away gives you a way out of a deal. You may find a better deal or discover something about this property that you really don't like.

ONE GOOD LOOPHOLE

You don't need a dozen ways out of a contract, just one good one. In all my years of buying, I have never used a loophole to get out of a deal. Make your offer good enough that you won't want out.

Sometimes small problems arise, or you discover something unexpected and expensive that's needed to fix the house. A loophole is not designed to protect you from little things, but major problems with that house or with you personally. It's like a major medical policy. When it comes to small issues, though, you should remember that every house has little things wrong with it and those issues may be part of the reason you are buying at a good price.

If you discover that the house you are buying has a problem that would be very expensive to correct, you will want to find a way to get out of the deal. Likewise, if you had a serious financial setback or personal disaster that would make closing problematic, you will want a way out of the deal.

A commonly accepted loophole is an inspection clause that allows you to unilaterally cancel the contract up to the closing date. Every house has something wrong with it. Most inspection clauses give the seller the right to correct the problem and close or to cancel the contract. You want a clause that obligates the seller to close but allows you to cancel the contract without giving a specific reason that could then be debated or corrected.

The clause could read, "The buyer has the right, at his expense, to inspect the house or to have the house inspected by a contractor or inspector; in the event that the buyer is not satisfied with the results, the buyer has the right to terminate this contract without further liability at any time before the closing." Have your attorney review and approve this clause before you use it.

When you buy a house at a good price, the seller is typically in a hurry to sell, and the reason you were able to get the good price is that you have agreed to close quickly. Most of my closings take place soon after I sign a contract. A contingency clause that ties up a property for months and gives the buyer the right to cancel the contract right up to the closing would not be acceptable to many sellers. Be wary of these clauses when you are selling.

AFTER YOU SIGN THE CONTRACT

After you and the seller sign the contract, make a copy for each party. If you have no way to make a copy, make two originals. Have the other party fill out a duplicate original by hand, proofread it carefully, and everyone sign both copies. You keep the one the seller filled out. It would be hard for the seller to claim that she did not understand the contract if she actually filled it out.

CONTRACTS CAN BE MODIFIED

If you need to change any provision of a printed or typed contract, you can by striking through the part that you want to change and writing the change near the part you struck through.

Make any changes clearly, striking through the number or conflicting language in the printed contract. Have all parties to the contract initial any changes, and if you use an addendum, have all parties sign and date it. If the change requires lengthy language, then using a separate addendum would be advisable.

USING A REALTOR'S CONTRACT WHEN BUYING THROUGH AN AGENT

Typically, when you are buying a property through an agent, the agent will want to use his contract. It will protect the agent and generally offers the seller, whom the agent represents, more protection than the buyer.

You can modify this contract to please you or you can use a separate addendum if you need to make changes or additions that won't fit on the contract. These Realtor contracts usually have a lot of fine print and little space to make additions or changes, so an addendum is a good way to add what you need to make the offer acceptable to you. Remember, both parties should strike through any words or phrases or complete sections that your addendum supersedes—and don't forget to initial it.

ADDENDUMS

Use a separate written addendum when many or lengthy modifications are required. If you use an addendum, have all parties (including the Realtor) sign and date it. The addendum should refer to the contract it is modifying.

For example, "This is an addendum to the contract between Joe and Sally Seller and Bob and Betty Buyer, dated January 5, 2016, regarding the property described as 123 Paradise Way, Sarasota, Florida."

You could add a complete legal description, but the address is sufficient because you will then attach the addendum to the full contract, which has a legal description.

Your addendum could include your inspection clause. It also may contain a clause dealing with existing loans and liens that you may want to keep on the property rather than pay them off at the closing.

ALWAYS BE WILLING TO WALK AWAY

No matter how well written your contract is, if one party wants out and won't close, it won't close. No matter how simple (or defective) your contract is, if both parties want to close, they will.

Suppose I reach an agreement with a seller and he changes his mind before closing and refuses to close. Even if I have the right to take him to court and force him to sell to me, is it worth the expense and amount of time required to do that?

The answer is, sometimes it is. If you have invested a lot of time and money in a property before the closing and will experience a large loss of profit if the sellers won't close, it may be worth suing them for specific performance. Recognize that this may cost you up-front attorney's fees and months, if not years, of your time. However, courts will enforce a contract, even if one side is making a large profit.

With a typical house purchase, it's not worth the time and money to sue to force the other side to close. It will be easier and faster to find another good deal than to force this one to close. Be confident that you can find another (and often better) deal and be willing to walk away with a smile.

If the seller has found another buyer who is willing to pay him more, ask the seller for part of the profit. It is better for the seller to pay you part of the profit than to go to court to resolve the problem.

If you willingly agree to cancel the contract rather than fight to keep them in the deal, sellers will sometimes change their minds. One seller called me to cancel a deal. I told her I'd be glad to because I had found another house I liked better. She then reconsidered and wanted me to close on her property.

IS A LONGER CONTRACT BETTER?

Is it easier for a homeowner to understand and agree to a twelve-page contract with a five-page addendum or a one-page agreement? Obviously, a shorter contract with less fine print is easier to understand and sellers are more likely to understand and sign it.

Use the shortest contract that gets the job done, and you will buy more property.

Realtors use a "form" contract prepared by their attorneys. When you buy through an agent, she will insist on using her contract, but that does not prevent you from adding to it or modifying it. Realtor/lawyer contracts have grown in size from one page (front and back) to twelve pages or more (front and back) during my time in the business. In addition to a twelve-page purchase, a sale agreement may include a five-page disclosure and another dozen pages of addendums that cover items not discussed in the contract.

Know what a contract requires and when it puts you in harm's way, then modify it so it protects you. Make your offers as clear and concise as possible and you will buy bargains that others miss.

SOME CONTRACT CLAUSES ARE ENFORCEABLE AFTER THE CLOSING

Parts of the contract may "survive" or be enforceable, even after the closing. A seller benefits by not having any continuing obligations or liabilities after the closing. When you are the seller, be aware of these potential ongoing obligations.

As a buyer, you would like the seller to be responsible if a problem, previously unknown to you, arises after the closing.

Common warranties and promises that a seller would make that would survive the closing are:

- Seller is conveying the property free of all mechanic's liens and other claims
- Seller warrants that information in the listing agreement, or otherwise provided, is correct to the best of his knowledge
- Seller warrants that he has disclosed to the buyer all material latent defects that are known to him
- Seller warrants that he has disclosed any information in his possession that materially and adversely affects the consideration paid by the buyer

In addition, the right to require specific performance (to force the other party to close as agreed in the contract) survives to both the buyer and seller, unless modified in the contract.

Although buyers commonly rely on representations made by agents, note this paragraph from a Realtor's contract:

> BUYER AGREES TO RELY SOLELY ON SELLER, PROFESSIONAL INSPECTORS, AND GOVERNMENTAL AGENCIES FOR VERIFICATION OF PROPERTY CONDITION, SQUARE FOOTAGE, AND FACTS THAT MATERIALLY AFFECT PROPERTY VALUE AND NOT ON THE REPRESENTATIONS (ORAL, WRITTEN, OR OTHERWISE) OF BROKER.

This paragraph puts buyers on notice not to rely on the agent's statements.

ASKING THE SELLER TO WRITE IT DOWN

When an offer is accepted by a seller in a hurry and he agreed to a price or terms favorable to you, have the seller write it down in its most basic form, to show that he understands the offer. "I, John Seller, accept Barb Buyer's offer to purchase my house at 2357 Prime Street, for a price of $100,000, with $10,000 down and the balance payable at $500 a month including interest of 3% until paid in full, closing on May 1, 2016. The buyers agree to pay all closing costs."

You can take a simple contract like this and fill in the blanks to reflect your understanding and all can sign it.

IN REVIEW

- A contract that will close will reflect a meeting of the minds. When both want to close they will do so and if either party does not want to close, it is better to look for another deal rather than try to force this deal to close.
- You never want to go to court; your contract does not have to be enforceable in a court. An agreement written on the back of an envelope will close if both parties want to close. Have a clear agreement that covers the important points and then close as soon as is practical. I often try to close in less than a week.

- Negotiate patiently and don't worry about losing the deal, but once you have an agreement, close quickly. If the sellers have agreed to sell to you at a bargain price or on good terms, someone else may offer them more. Closing sooner reduces this possibility.
- Filling out the contract is part of the negotiation process. Go slowly, one point at a time, and see how the seller reacts. You will learn a lot about how a seller negotiates. You can negotiate the points most important to you last, when you have a feel for how the seller negotiates.
- Always have a way out. Just one good loophole is all you need.
- Always be willing to walk away. Never make it personal. If they won't close, walking out of a closing sometimes brings them back to the table.

11

MAKING THE OFFER

TALK WITH THE SELLERS BEFORE YOU MAKE AN OFFER

After you have completed the Buying Strategy Worksheet (see Figure 4.1), sit down with the sellers and talk about what is important to them. You know what you are willing to pay. Now is the time to see if you can get an idea of *why* they are selling. The why may give you a clue as to how anxious they are to sell and how soon they need to sell.

Make sure that you are talking to the decision makers. If a husband and wife own the house, have both of them at the table. If there is another decision maker, such as a relative or an attorney, it is best to first make the deal with the sellers and then make that deal subject to review by the third party.

UNDERSTAND THE SELLERS' MOTIVATION BEFORE YOU MAKE THE OFFER

Ask the sellers, "Why are you selling such a nice house?" Then listen.

Write down on a blank sheet of paper what reason you think you heard them say is important to them. Then show it to them to see if you heard them correctly. This may include a fast closing, a certain amount of money that they need at closing to relocate or rent another house, the relief from their current monthly payments, or money for other obligations. If they have other obligations that are bothering them (e.g., credit card bills, student tuition due, and so on), have them list them.

There are two reasons to have them list these obligations:

1. Many times, they do not know exactly what they owe. One spouse may have borrowed money that the other spouse is not aware of.
2. There may be times when you can take the responsibility for paying off an obligation as part of your purchase price. If the seller owes money to a contractor, an attorney, a hospital, or a creditor whom he is not currently paying, you may be able to work out a repayment plan with the creditor. Instead of paying the creditor all cash, you can pay a monthly amount, often without interest. Sometimes a creditor will agree to take less than is owed.

TIPS FOR WHEN YOU ARE BUYING

Let the Seller Make the First "Offer"

When you are trying to get the best price, you want the other party to set his highest price first—before you make an offer. This will provide you with the most you will have to pay for a property. Sometimes it is a great price, and you won't have to negotiate. Typically, this number is close to a retail price or even higher.

House sellers often ask for more than they expect, hoping to get lucky. Setting a price too high is not a good selling strategy because it will turn off most buyers.

If you are the buyer, the price is only one of many things that you will negotiate. Some other items include the condition of the house, the personal property that will go with the house, the closing date, who will pay the closing costs, and the terms of any owner financing. You want to reach agreement on these and other issues that may come up, as part of the offer-making process.

Picking the Price for Your Offer

As the buyer, your offer should be at a low enough price or with such good terms that you will be very happy if the seller accepts. If you are not at least a little embarrassed by your first offer, you are offering too much. You should fall off your chair if they take it (and sometimes they do).

Plan ahead in order to make your offer good for you. Don't be overly concerned about what the sellers will accept. They will let you know if you are too low.

It is good strategy to ask for more than you really need to make the deal. The exception would be when buying from a distressed seller, which is covered later. Most sellers set the sales price a little high, anticipating that a buyer will make a lower offer. They may have a bottom-line price in mind.

Research what other comparable houses have sold for recently, and then compare the price of this house with those prices. Adjust the price for differences in condition or size, and then make your first offer below what you need to buy the house for to make a profit.

Suppose that a seller is asking for $250,000, and after researching the neighborhood you find that other comparable houses have sold for between $200,000 and $240,000 and that those houses were in better shape than the seller's. You determine that the seller's house is really worth between $200,000 and $220,000. Sometimes houses are on the market for years because they are overpriced. These houses can be opportunities, because the seller eventually becomes more motivated to sell and the market values catch up with her high price.

You decide that you would like to buy this house for about $175,000 and the owner wants $250,000. The house is vacant and needs cosmetic repairs and has been on the market for a year. Your first offer should be $160,000.

Offer Number One

NEVER, NEVER, NEVER try to think for the seller. Make your first offer an offer that you know will make you money and see how she responds. At $160,000 you know you have a bargain.

Offer Number Two

It often takes more than one offer to get an acceptance. The seller may counter your offer with a different price and terms you can counter back, or she could make a different offer entirely. How do you decide which approach to take?

If, after you make your first offer, the seller makes a big move in your direction, then stick with your strategy and move a little or sometimes not at all on your price and terms.

After your $160,000 offer, she tells you how much she has spent fixing up the house, and how the neighbors down the street just sold a smaller house for $275,000 (both fiction) then she counters with $225,000. By coming down $25,000 she shows that she is open to another offer, so you offer $165,000, but say that that is absolutely as high as you can go.

She wrings her hands and says that little Johnny will have to wait to go to college and counters with her final offer of $200,000. You thank her for compromising but say that this is the most you have ever paid for a house in this neighborhood. However, you are willing to split the difference with her and pay $175,000 if she will include the appliances. She sighs and agrees.

Offer Number Three

However, what if after your first offer, she counters at $245,000? With that small of a move she is unlikely to get down to your price. So take a different approach. Offer her $175,000 with $10,000 down and the balance payable at $1,000 a month, including 3 percent interest. That gives her a higher interest rate than she can earn in a bank.

You would have researched the income and expenses, and would know that the house will produce a net income of conservatively $1,100 a month, giving you a very acceptable $100 a month cash flow on your $10,000 investment.

Stop and think about these last two offers. If you could have either one accepted today, which would you choose? ***Whichever you choose, make that type of offer first, next time.*** For a full day of negotiation strategies, study my course "Negotiation Secrets of a Professional Buyer" (further details on this can be found on my website www.johnschaub.com). You can always improve as a negotiator, and improving pays well.

Don't Let a Seller Shop Your Offer

When a seller uses your offer to solicit a higher offer from someone else, it is called *shopping your offer*. While this is good for the seller, it's not good for you. Real estate brokers who represent the seller will sometimes try to get two buyers to bid against each other to get the seller a higher price and to earn a higher commission.

You can avoid people shopping your offer by making an offer that has to be accepted or rejected in a short period of time. An offer can contain a clause that states that the seller must respond by a certain time and date, for example by "5:00 p.m. on July 1, 2016." If you are making an offer directly to a seller, ask him or her before you make the offer, "Are you ready to sell your house today?"—then make an offer. The seller needs to accept it or make a counteroffer now (or within a few hours). *Never give sellers several days to think it over.* They will use those days to get a higher offer from someone else.

Tell the sellers that the offer is good today and today only. If they don't accept, your offer is off the table. If they come back to you later and want to sell, you can reconsider, but you won't guarantee to pay this much.

You can add strength to this statement by telling them about another house you are looking at and saying that you cannot afford to buy them both. Tell them that you like their house better and are making them your first offer, but if they don't accept it, you will then try to buy the other house.

Counteroffers

Dee Fountain was a successful agent who insisted that a seller make a counteroffer and did it with a smile so that the sellers were encouraged to make some concession to keep the deal alive. "Don't tell me what you won't do; tell me what you will do."

When a seller refuses your offer ask, "Would you buy this house today for what I am offering you?" If he turns down your offer, he has, in effect, just bought his house for that amount—he could have had your money instead of his house.

Never Give a Seller a Big Deposit

When you make an offer, you typically show that you are serious by including a deposit with the contract. Do not give the seller this deposit. Make your check out to an attorney or title company who will handle the closing.

If you need to gain creditability with the sellers by showing them that you have the money necessary to buy their house, you could bring a cashier's check payable to your attorney or title company with you and attach it to your offer.

This check does not need to be for the full down payment. A check for $1,000 should be enough to show that you are serious.

If you are agreeing to close within a short period of time—a week or two—agree to make the deposit with the attorney or title company within forty-eight hours after they have accepted your offer. If you are signing a contract on a weekend, you typically have to wait until Monday morning before you can give the attorney or title company your check.

This gives you time to raise the down payment if you don't have the money, and a way out of the deal if you change your mind. The language in your offer will determine who gets the earnest money and what happens with it in the event that either the buyer or the seller fails to close.

Use language that protects you. The contract may state that you are entitled to a refund of your deposit if you don't close because of certain reasons; for instance, an inability to finance the property. It may state that the sellers can keep your deposit as liquidated damages if you don't close, but that is all that they can have and that you have no other liability. The language in a broker's contract is more likely to favor the seller and the broker over the potential buyer.

If a real estate agent is involved, the agent will want to hold the deposit. Give the agent the smallest amount possible. One hundred dollars is sufficient if you are agreeing to close in a week or two. Both the seller and the broker will want more deposit money if the closing date is months away.

HOW TO USE A HOME INSPECTOR AS A SAFETY NET

Hiring a home inspector to give a potential purchase a good look is a great idea. A home inspector should check out all the major systems, such as plumbing, electrical, heat/air conditioning, and the structure and roof. Meet him at the house, and walk around with him. Don't pester him with too many questions, but watch him work and learn from watching. You will learn a few tricks that you can use yourself.

He will give you a written report that you then can use to negotiate with the seller in the event that you find a previously undisclosed problem with the house. If you have already negotiated a great deal, don't be foolish and ask for more if the problems you discover are small. Your counteroffer will let him out of the obligation to sell to you, and he may then sell to another buyer for more money.

Instead of negotiating over small items, use the home inspection as an insurance policy against major problems that you might otherwise miss. If you are having second thoughts about buying the house after reading the inspection, this means that you have not made a great deal and that you should ask for more concessions from the seller. If this does happen, you should be willing to risk the deal getting away.

HOW TO HANDLE A SELLER WHO WANTS A THIRD PARTY TO APPROVE A CONTRACT

Sometimes a seller will want his or her attorney or a family member to look over or approve a contract. Often this is done because the seller does not understand the contract. This is why you should try to make your offers as simple as possible.

If the seller still insists on having a third party involved, use language that keeps the deal together, unless the third party can introduce new information that influences the seller's decision. For example, with an attorney, insert a clause that says, "This transaction will close as agreed unless Attorney [enter the attorney's name] notifies both the buyer and seller in writing within three days stating how the contract is not in compliance with current statutes and regulations."

Never say that it is "subject to the approval" of an attorney or anyone else. No attorney would ever put his stamp of approval on anything that might subject him to liability.

DEALING WITH OWNERS WHO ARE NOT AT THE TABLE

If you are negotiating with one party in a divorce, one heir to an estate, or one partner in a partnership that is splitting up, then make your offer subject to being able to buy out the other party on terms agreeable to you. This will be a totally separate negotiation. You can pay a different price or buy on different terms. With a property that has multiple owners in title, often one will need cash today and will be willing to accept less money if he or she gets it now. Another owner will hold out for a higher price but be willing to accept terms.

Although these negotiations take more time, they also have more potential for profit. Of course, you need to make any purchase of a partial interest subject to being able to buy the rest of the property. A partial interest is hard to sell, and it can be expensive to force another partial owner to sell.

FOUR SECRETS TO GETTING YOUR OFFER ACCEPTED

Sellers are more likely to accept an offer that they understand, gives them instant or near-instant gratification, and requires them to do little work.

1. *First, keep your offer simple.* Avoid long, complicated contracts. Sellers will refuse to sign them simply because they can't understand them. Sellers need to know how much money they are going to get and when they are going to get it. Be as specific and clear as possible on these two points.

2. *Second, make a net offer with you paying all the closing costs.* Know what your closing costs will be, and calculate them into your offer. This gives the seller the answer to "How much money will I get?"

3. *Third, offer to buy the house in "as is" condition.* This allows the seller to leave the house without doing any work. By taking all the risk, you can increase your profit. Of course, you need to either inspect the house thoroughly before you make the offer or make the inspection a contingency in your contract. Even with an "as is" offer, you can require the seller to leave the house in its current condition, without further damage. Walk through the house before you close to make sure that it is in the same condition as it was when you inspected it. If there is additional damage, you can renegotiate the price to compensate for it.

4. *Finally, offer to close quickly.* Sellers will often accept lower offers that close sooner. They are selling because they need money now. If they could wait, they could sell for more.

If you can incorporate all these items into your offers, you will buy more houses and further below the market.

The checklist that follows will take you step by step through the process of finding, negotiating, and closing your first deal. Use it for every house you buy.

Making the Offer

1. Identify a potential bargain purchase; ask questions.
2. Write down the one urgent problem you can solve for the seller.
3. Establish the fair market value, give or take 5 percent.
4. Research the market rent and likely net income the property will produce.
5. State your minimum acceptable profit on this house.
6. Formulate an offer that solves the seller's one urgent problem.
7. Make the offer. Insist on either an acceptance or a counteroffer. (Remember: *Don't tell me what you won't do; tell me what you will do.*)
8. Make another offer based on any new information.
9. If the seller is unresponsive but you remain convinced there is opportunity, go away and come back in a week with another offer.
10. Get the contract accepted and signed by all parties.
11. Make your earnest money deposit with the closing agent.
12. Retain rights to use a house inspector and termite inspector, if needed.
13. Order a title search with a title company, attorney, or escrow company, and furnish these agents with a copy of your fully signed contract.
14. Talk with the agent or attorney who will prepare the closing documents to alert him or her to any unusual clauses in the contract.
15. Get copies of any documents you will be required to sign the day before the closing, and get a copy of the title insurance commitment—read them to check for exceptions.
16. Read closing documents (very carefully!).
17. Walk through the house the day of the closing, after the sellers are completely out of the house.
18. Go to the closing, review the documents, and collect the appropriate items listed on the closing documents list, and get the keys and garage door opener.

Note: When you are buying, take your time. Time is on your side. Having both the buyers and the sellers at the closing can work to your advantage. When you are selling, sign documents in advance. Only go to pick up your check after the buyer has signed everything and left.

12

SECRETS OF PROFESSIONAL NEGOTIATORS

You are a negotiator—we all are. Some are better than others because they have learned from their experience how others react to certain offers. You can level the playing field with these good negotiators by recognizing their techniques and being prepared for any negotiation that involves a lot of money.

A penny saved is a penny earned.

—Benjamin Franklin

I suspect that Benjamin Franklin was an excellent negotiator. He understood that saving a penny when you buy something is the equivalent of earning that same penny—and that was before we had an income tax.

Today, when you save $10,000 because you buy something at a below-market price, you have saved even more than the discount you made. To pay the extra dollar to buy something, you first have to earn that dollar plus the tax you owe on it. Saving $10,000 when you buy something is the equivalent of earning the $10,000 plus tax.

Real estate investors understand this concept and use their skills to buy properties at large discounts that are tax-free to the buyers unless they decide to sell.

Two of my students use this idea to significantly reduce the amount of tax they pay while at the same time increasing their yearly "profits." These high-income individuals choose to reduce the number of hours they work at their normal professions. This reduces their taxable earned income and taxes that they owe.

They then use the time they are not working at their jobs to buy property at bargain prices. They may earn $100,000 working "part-time" and then buy several properties at a discount of even more than $100,000 during the hours that they spend as buyers. The discount they earn is untaxed until they sell the property, if ever. Plus, the properties they buy grow in value, untaxed until they sell.

LEARNING TO BECOME A FAIR BUT GOOD NEGOTIATOR

If you are going to buy, sell, and manage real estate, then you need to learn to negotiate. As you become good at it, you will make a lot more money. Negotiation is probably the most valuable skill that you can acquire.

Negotiating has a bad reputation. It is not the art of taking advantage of someone else. It is the art of putting a deal together.

An important element in negotiating for a house, especially one that you would like to buy with owner financing, is developing trust with the seller. If you are truthful in your statements, if you don't try to manipulate him with emotional statements, he will then be more willing to trust you as you negotiate.

Some sellers never sell because they have no skills in getting a buyer to commit to buy, even when it would be very good for the buyer. Landlords have vacant houses because they never get potential tenants to commit to renting.

Negotiating is a skill you can acquire, although many people seem to be born with it. Take a three-year-old to a store and you will experience how a persistent negotiator, one who won't take no for an answer, can get what he wants.

There are several secrets that successful negotiators use to reach an agreement. Notice I did not say to *win*, but to reach an agreement. Unless both parties to a negotiation receive some benefit, the deal generally will fall apart, with one party failing to perform as agreed.

ONE-SIDED DEALS OFTEN FALL APART BEFORE CLOSING

An example of a failed negotiation is when a salesperson uses an emotional argument to get a buyer to sign a contract. Such a close might be that this house is offered way below the market value and that another buyer is on his way over to sign a contract. If you want to buy it, you need to make an offer right now, or it will be gone.

After a contract is signed under this kind of pressure, the buyer may check out other houses for sale and learn that the house that he bought was not a bargain. He would then do what he could to get out of the contract, using excuses such as a lack of financing or deficiencies in the property for not buying.

Another example is a buyer who drives a hard bargain with a builder and negotiates such a good price that the builder cannot build the house at a profit. The builder may then cut corners during the construction, delivering an inferior house, or simply refuse to build the house.

Some people are quick to hire an attorney to enforce their rights under a one-sided contract. The argument is that once everyone agreed, then every party should be forced to comply. Hiring an attorney and going to court to enforce a contract, however, is rarely a profitable adventure.

If you find that you have negotiated a one-sided deal and determine that the other party cannot perform reasonably, then reopen the negotiations. See if you can negotiate a deal that will work. If you consider the cost of both sides hiring an attorney and going to court, it is far cheaper to give a few dollars on each side to make the deal work. In addition, going to court will delay your closing and take a lot of your time. The total cost makes suing someone to enforce a contract that was one-sided to begin with an expensive misadventure.

There are many approaches you can take to a negotiation. Figure 12.1 presents four examples of results that are somewhat predictable, depending on the approach that you take.

Here are outcomes for each of these types of negotiations:

FIGURE 12.1   Negotiation Matrix

I Win/You Lose	You Lose/I Lose
You Win/I Lose	I Win/You Win

I Win/You Lose

You are buying from a seller who is short on time and resources and must sell. You make the seller a low "take it or leave it" offer. The seller takes it but goes away mad.

Another example may be when you are dealing with another professional negotiator, such as a lawyer, a banker, or a Realtor. You know you have the advantage and use it to make a profit. It's not personal, just business. An example may be when you find a property in foreclosure and recognize that a bank will lose a significant amount of money unless it makes a deal today. You make the bank a low offer, which it accepts for a small loss but recovers most of the money it loaned.

You Lose/I Lose

When one party in the negotiation has most of the power, typically the party with the money, then that party can overleverage the other party by making an offer that so offends the other party that he won't take it or continue negotiations. A "take it or leave it" low offer to a homeowner who is behind in his payments is an example.

You Win/I Lose

Sometimes it is wise to lose a negotiation. I had a long-term tenant call me to ask if I would pay for half the cost of the paint if he would provide the labor to repaint the interior of several rooms. I said no, that I would not pay for half the paint—I would pay for it all if the tenant would use my favorite color, antique white.

I often "lose" negotiations with good customers that I could easily win, because by losing I enhance our long-term relationship, and that relationship is often very profitable.

I Win/You Win

When a seller is under a lot of pressure to sell, you make her an offer that allows you to make a reasonable profit but leaves her enough money to move and rent another home to live in, and you also give her the time to move.

QUESTIONS TO ASK BEFORE YOU NEGOTIATE

1. Is the person with whom I am negotiating able to make a binding decision? If not, ask who can make that final decision and negotiate with that person.

With smaller transactions, such as a purchase at a store or when borrowing money at a bank or buying a car, you typically are dealing with an employee, not an owner. The owner would have authority to negotiate and make a binding decision. An employee may have some negotiating authority but typically will seek approval before making a commitment.

When borrowing from a bank, the banker who interviews you when you apply for a loan may give you the indication that he will make you the loan, but typically he will need the approval of the loan committee, which may be a committee of one, the boss. Bankers typically have a certain *loan authority*, the amount that they are authorized to lend without further approval. The higher you move up in the bank hierarchy, the larger the loan authority, until at some level a real committee would approve the transaction.

When you are buying or selling a house, you are often dealing with a married couple or sometimes two partners who own a house together. The decision to buy or sell is typically a joint decision, and you need to involve both parties in the negotiation, because they both will have to sign the contract. One person may be the decision maker. When you identify the decision maker (it may not be the one doing all of the talking), ask him or her what it would take to make a deal today.

2. Is it worth my time to negotiate? Although some people consider it fun to negotiate for everything, rather than trying to talk a store clerk into giving you a discount on a loaf of

bread, save your energy for the purchase where you can save several dollars or hundreds or thousands of dollars.

> *Once you reach fifty, you should not have to negotiate for everything.*
> —*Jimmy Buffett,* **A Pirate Turns Fifty**

Most day-to-day negotiations involve little potential to make a profit. Plan ahead to be well prepared for the bigger negotiations that are worth hundreds or thousands of dollars to you. By being prepared for the big negotiations, you will profit considerably, allowing you to follow Jimmy Buffett's advice.

3. How will this negotiation affect my relationship with this person/company, and are future negotiations with this person/company likely to be important?

Many negotiations lead to another negotiation. The first interaction sets the stage for the second. Those with whom you negotiate can be a source of referrals—or result in lost business. If you aim to be a long-term success in your business, then positive referrals can be a large part of your business.

When you rent to a tenant, the tenant has the potential to be a source of income to you for a long time. The tenant also may refer other friends to you or steer others away from you. How you negotiate with this tenant will affect how she treats your house and what she tells others about you as a landlord.

Many of my tenants have been referred to me by other tenants. This is not because I am a pushover but because I deliver a good house at a fair price, and I'm predictable in how I respond to tenant requests. McDonald's has built a billion-dollar business not because its food is the cheapest or even the tastiest, but because its food is predictable. You know what you are going to get. I have built my tenant management business using the same principle. Fair and predictable. No surprises. It works.

4. Is this the best time and place to negotiate?

When you are the buyer, you get to choose when and where to negotiate the purchase. You want to be well prepared and in good shape both physically and mentally before you begin the negotiation.

Have a good meal, be well rested, and take plenty of time to think through what you plan to say. Only when you are at your best and well prepared should you negotiate for tens of thousands of dollars.

You want to have a plan. If things are not going according to your plan, take a break and regroup. When you are the buyer, you are in control of the situation. Walking away and then starting again can work in your favor as the buyer. The seller will see you as a serious buyer when you come back, and you can pick up the negotiation where you left off last time.

Although I close some properties within a week, I often take weeks, and occasionally months, to buy other properties. I visit with the owners a number of times, and each meeting moves me a little closer toward my goal.

WHERE TO NEGOTIATE

When you are buying a family's home, it is better to negotiate the purchase somewhere other than in the home—for many reasons. The first reason is distractions. Their home is full of distractions, from kids and pets to perhaps the neighbors dropping by.

If you are going to make an offer in their home, you need to take charge of the situation and eliminate as many distractions as possible. One of my students is a very successful buyer and often buys sitting at the seller's kitchen table. To eliminate distractions, he first pulls the FOR SALE sign out of the yard and puts it alongside the house. Once inside, he takes charge of the situation by turning off the TV and asking the sellers to turn off their cell phones. He wants to reduce the distractions while he is buying the house. If the sellers object to this, he knows that they don't want to sell to him that day.

I prefer to ask the sellers to meet me outside their home. I ask them to bring their file on the home, including their purchase documents, current insurance and tax bills, and a current loan statement. This is asking a lot of these possible sellers, and it is a test.

If the sellers are only mildly interested in selling, then they will decline my offer. If they really want to sell, they will meet me with all their information. Because I am a wholesale buyer, I only want to meet with sellers who are ready to sell and need to sell now.

Look for an office you might have access to because of other business that you do, such as a conference room at a bank or a title or escrow company.

This more professional setting has advantages over a coffee shop, such as copy machines, but a coffee shop can work. When I teach classes on buying property, my students actually find sellers and make them offers. Many of those offers have been made in coffee shops or 24-hour restaurants, and hundreds of successful negotiations are concluded there.

BEFORE YOU NEGOTIATE

Secrets of Professional Negotiators

1. *Know the value before you make an offer.* Based on the rental survey you conducted, you will know how much rent the prospective tenants will pay and therefore how much you can afford to borrow and repay if you buy this house. You also will have tracked comparable houses that have sold and be able to establish a price range within 10 percent.

2. *Negotiate for the things that are least important to you first.* You may begin by negotiating for the appliances. If the sellers won't agree to include the appliances, you may adjust your strategy to continue to ask for several minor items, such as making repairs to the house or a delayed closing date. It's okay to lose on these issues, but wait to negotiate the issues that are more important to you last. At that point, you have reached agreement on many issues, and the sellers will have a lot of time and emotion invested in selling you their house. You can use the momentum created because you have made concessions to conclude the negotiation at a price and on terms acceptable to you.

3. *Invoke the doctrine of fairness.* One of the best negotiators I know is Jim Napier. One of his favorite negotiating techniques is to raise the issue of fairness when it appears that one party is taking unfair advantage of the situation. An example might be when one party continues to prevail on every issue. After one side wins on several issues, it only seems fair that the other side should win something. Jimmy would ask, "Is that fair?" When they asked for an explanation he would review all the points of negotiation that he had conceded on and then ask "Is it fair that if you get to name the price that I get to name the terms?"

   By negotiating with a plan, you can strategically lose many issues that are less important to you, holding out for the one item that is critical to you in the negotiation. It might be the price, the down payment, or the terms of the financing.

After you spend considerable time negotiating seriously with the sellers, they become confident that you will buy their house. After you have reached agreement on many points, it is time to negotiate the point or points most important to you. Now you can invoke the doctrine of fairness, if necessary, reciting all the concessions that you have made to try to put this deal together.

4. ***Never bid against yourself.*** I once sold a house at an auction. There were only a few serious bidders, and one bidder got so excited about buying the house that he bid twice in a row. He bid $65,000, and when no one else acted, he made another bid of $70,000. He raised his own bid, bidding against himself.

You may think that this seems funny, but during actual negotiations for a major purchase, such as a house, it is very exciting—and it is easy to raise your own bid. It generally happens when the other party just does not respond to your offer.

Silence can be a powerful tool. If you offer the sellers a price for their house and they simply don't respond, what is your reaction? Typically, it is to offer more. A seller who understands this can get you to bid against yourself.

I once bought a property from Jim Napier. I made him an offer, and he just looked at me. He said nothing, but I thought his look conveyed that he did not think that the offer was good enough. After what seemed like a long time, I asked him what he thought would be a fair price. He still did not respond, so eventually I offered him a little more, trying to get him to engage in negotiation. His silence eventually forced me to bid against myself. It's a powerful tool, but it takes some practice before you can use it effectively.

5. ***How to negotiate with an agent.*** The best deals I have ever made have been brought to me by agents. In Chapter 13 you will learn how to negotiate with and through an agent.

6. ***When there are two or more sellers and they are hostile to each other.*** When there is a divorce or another partnership that is breaking up on less-than-friendly terms, you need to negotiate with the parties separately. Sometimes, when an estate is settled, several heirs will end up with a property. They may not even know each other, but it is almost certain that they will have different needs and demands. One may need

cash right away and will sell quickly to get it, whereas another will want a higher price and be willing to wait for it.

This can become an advantage to a buyer when handled carefully. Anything you say to one party may be communicated to another party, so you want to take the high ground and never disparage the other parties, even though the person you are with may have a lot of ugly things to say.

Your job when dealing with multiple sellers is to find out what each one needs and when and then to structure an offer to buy just the one share on those terms. Then approach the other, or another, heir as noted in the preceding section on multiple owners.

A twenty-something heir may want quick cash to buy a new car or take a vacation. You could agree to buy his share at a wholesale price and close quickly. An older heir may want a higher price but be willing to accept payment for her share over a number of years to supplement her retirement income. A third heir may want to occupy the property for a time or even keep an interest in the property, thinking that it will be worth substantially more in a few years. You can make a separate deal with all three.

7. ***Getting on the same team with the other party.*** Have you ever made an offer to buy a car from a dealer and have the salesperson leave you to get the approval of his sales manager? What happened? Typically, the salesperson returns with the bad news that he could not give you that much for your trade-in car or that he could not sell the new car to you for that little, and then he will try to talk you out of more of your money.

   He blames the other party (in this case his manager) for the higher price and tries to befriend you. He will work hard for you to try to get you the best deal he can.

   Notice this technique, because it is one of the best negotiating strategies. Rather than set up an adversarial relationship with the buyer (you), the salesperson puts his arm around you (figuratively, if not literally) and becomes your ally in this battle against the sales manager.

   Together, as a team, you will come up with a strategy that the sales manager will accept. The salesperson will become your knight in shining armor and do battle with the enemy until you finally prevail.

   In the end, the salesperson will congratulate you on being a tough negotiator and for making a great deal. You will go away thinking that you really made a good deal and feel good about your purchase. That is the way a successful negotiation should end.

You don't have to worry about the car dealer going out of business. They are professionals, and before they started talking with you, they knew the lowest offer that they would take for the car you bought. Their process is geared toward getting you to pay more than their lowest number.

I took my son with me the last time I bought a car and told him what was going to happen at each step of the negotiation. He was pretty impressed that I knew almost exactly what the salesperson would say and what techniques he would use.

Buying a car is actually pretty predictable. The salespeople have done it hundreds of times and know what works and what doesn't. The next time you buy a car, pay attention to the salesperson's technique, and rather than playing the role he expects, have a little fun. On a slow day, it can be fun and good practice to drop by a dealership and negotiate to buy a car even if you don't really want to buy one. If it's a slow day at the dealership, the salespeople will be happy for a little practice themselves, and if they are good, they may make you a deal you can't refuse. Be careful, unless you want a new car.

The next time you buy a car, do something unexpected, and see how the salesperson reacts. After the salesperson comes back with the bad news from the sales manager, rather than increase your bid, ask to use the phone and call somebody. Call a competing car salesperson whose card you brought with you and explain the deal. I guarantee you that that salesperson will promise you a better deal.

Now give your car salesperson one more chance to reduce the price rather than increasing yours. Be nice. Tell the salesperson that you would rather do business with him because you do like his car and his dealership better. Turn the tables on him, and get him to bid against himself.

If he tells you that he can't do any better, thank him for his time and stand up and start to walk out. Before you hit the door, he will ask you to give him one more chance to get his manager to meet your price. If he thinks that you are ready to buy that day, he won't let you leave without doing his best to make a deal.

If you are in the business of buying or selling something and you have a real customer who wants to do business with you, you don't want that customer to walk away without making a deal. Buyers or sellers who walk away often make a deal with someone else. When you find yourself with a seller who needs to sell or a buyer or prospective tenant who likes your property, work hard to make the deal now. If they leave to think it over, you rarely will see them again.

8. ***Know when to walk away.*** Some sellers are in so much trouble that you may not be able to buy their property even though they desperately need to sell. One seller had several young children, and her spouse had walked out on her. She was months behind in her payments and desperate for some cash to move into a rental property. The lenders would not cooperate, so she had no equity in her house, and there was no profit potential for an investor.

In cases like this it is tempting to pay the seller too much for her house, just to help her out. What this seller needs is charity, not for you to pay too much for her house. If you truly want to help, write her a check for moving expenses, but don't buy her house for too much money. Try not to confuse business with charity. Make money in your business operation, and then be generous with your charitable gifts. There are a lot of people who need your help.

NEGOTIATIONS AND NEGOTIATORS TO AVOID

Not everyone plays by the same rules. Some people will do anything to win a negotiation, including lying and outright stealing. It is foolish to think that you can outsmart these people or that you can keep them honest even with a great contract.

Avoid negotiating with people you find to be dishonest. Even if they agree to a deal, they will not honor their agreement. They will either refuse to close, or they will start negotiating all over again.

The great majority of people are honest, and once they have reached an agreement, they will perform as they agreed. If you find yourself dealing with a dishonest person, walk away. It will save you both time and money.

WHEN A DEAL IS GOOD ENOUGH, QUIT NEGOTIATING AND BUY

One of the best buyers I ever met was Jack Miller, who said it this way: "Don't steal in slow motion."

If a seller is ready to make you a great deal on his property, stop negotiating! Don't ask for anything more; just accept his offer. To do this, you need to be ready to buy. You need to know what the property is worth, know how to fill out a contract, and know how you will pay for the property.

The best deals happen quickly. Selling and buying a house are as much emotional decisions as business decisions. The day the sellers decide to get rid of the house and move on, they will make some buyer a good deal. If you happen to be in the right place at the right time, that could be you, if you have the ability to make the deal right then.

13

BUYING AND SELLING WITH AGENTS

S ome of your best buys will be through licensed real estate agents. There is a misconception that agents buy all the good listings. It's not true. In fact, any informed agent knows that it is a conflict of interest to buy his own listing. An agent does not represent his client's best interest by buying that client's property at a bargain price.

I use the term *agent* rather than *Realtor* here because the term *Realtor* is a registered trademark of the National Association of Realtors and refers only to its members. While only some agents are Realtors, all Realtors are agents.

ENTICING AGENTS TO CALL YOU WITH GOOD DEALS

How can you convince agents to call you when they find a good deal? Use the carrot-and-stick approach. The carrot: Tell the agent that if she brings you a listing that meets your criteria, you always will make an offer. Now, for that offer to be good for the agent, the buyer has to put enough down to pay the commission.

Carefully explain what you are looking for. Tell agents that you are looking for an empty house or a house owned by sellers who need to sell this week. Anyone who owns an empty house is getting no benefit from it and probably is worrying about it. These sellers are the most motivated to sell.

BUYING BIGGER EQUITIES

When I started my investment career, I would look for houses where the price listed was the loan balance plus the commission. My reasoning was that these sellers probably were having trouble making their payments, because they would get nothing from the sale but relief from the loan. When I made offers on these houses, there was never enough money to pay a full commission.

There are two weaknesses with this strategy. First, you rarely buy much below the market. Second, the agent doesn't remember you fondly because it is unlikely that she was paid a full commission for the sale.

A better strategy is to tell agents that you are looking for houses with bigger equities. This will give you more room to negotiate a better price, and it increases the chance that the agent would get paid a full commission.

Stress that you have the ability to make a quick decision and could close the sale in a week or less. This will get you a lot of calls in the last days of the listing period (a great time to make an offer—both the seller and the agent are under pressure to make a deal).

The stick in the carrot-and-stick approach is this: Tell agents that when you find a desperate seller and the agent with the listing has not called you, then the offer may not include enough cash to pay the commission. This is subtle, but they get it.

WHO TO CALL WHEN YOU WANT TO BUY A LISTING

Most of us know a number of real estate brokers and salespeople. When you spot a house or an ad for a house that has potential, it is a mistake to call a friend. If they want to get paid, they should be looking for these deals and calling *you*.

When you find a potential bargain, call the listing agent. The agent will receive two shares of the commission if she sells her own listing. This extra incentive to put the deal together will have this agent working twice as hard to get it closed.

I made a $170,000 offer on a house listed for $225,000. I eventually raised my offer to $175,000, still short of what the seller needed to pay off the loan and pay closing costs. The listing agent agreed to pitch in part of her commission to make the deal work.

PAYING AGENTS WHEN THERE IS NO CASH FOR A COMMISSION

Sometimes there is not enough cash in the transaction to pay a commission. Most residential brokers are hoping for a check at the closing. When there is no money to pay them a cash commission, promise to pay them later, perhaps when you resell the property. You can back your promise to pay with a promissory note secured by either the property you are buying or another property that you already own.

The top agents in any town make a lot of money. They avoid investing because it is too much trouble. If you make investing easy for them, you may be able to turn things around and collect a check from them at the closing rather than write them one. Look at your agent as a possible investor. Even if they don't have the money today, you flatter them by asking them.

Keep in mind that in a normal market, 60 to 70 percent of listings expire before they sell. If the agent is convinced that this one will not sell, he will be eager to make some deal to get paid something for his efforts, advertising, and so on.

One thing Warren Harding taught me was to follow the cash in a transaction. Agents often buy a gift for the new buyer and stay in touch with him. Wrong strategy. The buyer is broke. He just spent it all on the house. Stay in touch with the seller or the agent. They have cash in their pocket and may be potential investors, and the agent may bring you a deal.

BUYING ON LEASE OPTIONS THROUGH AGENTS

Often the best offer to make on a house is to lease it with an option to buy. How do you pay the broker when you are making a low down payment such as an option payment? Offer to pay the agent part of the fee when the lease/option agreement is signed and the balance at the actual closing.

You can go a step further and say to the agent and the seller that if you do not close on the purchase, the seller would agree to relist the property with the same agent when the option expires. In this way, the agent gets part of a commission now and will get another full commission when he sells it again.

Suppose that a house is listed for $140,000, and you offer to lease it for four years, paying $5,000 down as option consideration today. A 7 percent commission is $9,800. If the agent received 25 percent of that commission, or $2,450 today, with the balance paid when you exercise the option, this is still far better than not selling the house at all. If the seller is more anxious than the agent, then the agent may negotiate for more of the option payment.

USING THE DIFFERENT TYPES OF LISTINGS

The two commonly used types of listings are an *open listing* and *an exclusive right of sale.* An open listing is typically unwritten. With an open listing, the owner agrees to pay the broker only if she produces a sale, while the owner reserves the right to sell it herself without paying a commission. If another agent sells it, only that agent is entitled to a commission.

An exclusive listing guarantees the agent a commission if the property sells during the term of the listing regardless of who sells it. Exclusive listings are required by Multiple Listing Systems (MLS) and many of the big brokers. Many exclusive listings can obligate a seller to pay a commission to the agent if anyone they showed the house to (or even told about it) buys the house within a specified period after the listing expires. Read these listings carefully before you sign one or make an offer on a house bound by one.

A seller can exclude specific buyers, even from an exclusive listing. If you are interested in a house that a seller is going to list with an agent, have the seller exclude you from that listing. Then, if you buy, there will be no obligation to pay a commission.

Another type of listing, the *exclusive agency listing,* allows the owner to avoid paying a commission if he sells it himself but protects one agent in the event another agent sells it. It is not used as commonly because MLS generally will not accept properties listed this way.

If you ever list a property, use an exclusive listing to get the benefit of MLS exposure. You want every hotshot selling agent in town showing your house. Agree to pay the highest commission common in your area. The difference between 6 and 7 percent is not as important as selling the house quickly.

Insist on a short-term agreement. A ninety-day listing is as long as I would suggest. Read the fine print carefully, and remember to exclude any buyers with whom you are now negotiating. Be wary of accepting offers that are subject to the buyers obtaining financing or selling another house before they close on yours. These offers take your house off the market without compensation to you. If you do want to accept an offer subject to one of these contingencies, use one of these strategies:

1. State that in the event that you receive another offer acceptable to you, the buyers will have the right to waive their contingency and close within thirty days or void the contract.
2. Ask for a nonrefundable deposit of $1,000 that the buyers forfeit if they fail to close. This money will compensate you for taking the property off the market for a month. If the buyers need longer than thirty days, ask for more deposit money.

AGENTS CAN BE GOOD CUSTOMERS

Not all agents are rolling in dough. In fact, only the top producers make any serious money. Most are average consumers, struggling to pay their mortgage and car payments. I have both sold houses to and bought houses from such agents.

Many agents have trouble qualifying for a loan because their income is from commissions and is not predictable. In addition, some have credit problems. They are good candidates for a lease/option or owner-financing sale. Recently, I sold two houses that needed quite of bit of work to agents on lease/options. They can fix them up and then refinance them and pay me off.

I've bought many homes from agents. One agent has sold me his personal residence twice. When times are good, he buys a nice home, but he never gets emotionally attached to it. When cash gets tight, he knows that I will buy it and gives me a call. He knows that when he can't borrow, he can sell.

As you develop trust with agents, they become repeat customers. They will bring you sellers or buyers and sometimes just refer business to you. An agent can't make money from a buyer who has little money or credit. But that buyer may make a good tenant for you or even a lease/option buyer.

Likewise, an agent can't collect a commission from a seller who is behind on her payments and has no equity. However, you may know how to buy that house, save the seller's credit, and make a profit. I have had several calls referring these desperate sellers to me by agents.

ADVICE TO AGENTS WHO BUY PROPERTY

If you are an agent, *don't* buy your own listings. You are the agent for the seller and cannot ethically make a good deal. Cancel any and all listings, whether written or implied, before making an offer. If you buy your own listing and either deduct your commission or receive it at the closing and later resell the property for a profit, you are likely to be sued by the seller. The seller will claim that all you are entitled to is a commission, but you made more. Therefore, the seller is entitled to the overage (plus attorney's fees and costs).

Don't pay taxes on your own money. When you make a down payment and then collect a commission at the closing, you are just getting part of your down payment back. Unfortunately, any commission you receive is taxable income to you.

Likewise, if you trade services for a down payment, the services you trade can be classified as taxable income. If you forgo a commission and take equity in the property, you have still earned that commission, and it is still taxable. When buying, do not participate in any commission.

SHOULD YOU HAVE A REAL ESTATE LICENSE?

If all you do is buy for your own investment, the license is not necessary or even an advantage. An agent must disclose that he is licensed when making offers. I never found this to be a problem, although others have. A typical disclosure may read: "John Smith is a registered real estate broker in the state of Florida and is purchasing this property for his own account with the intention of making a profit. Smith will not participate in any commissions paid in this transaction. Any listing, whether written, oral, or implied, between Smith and the seller is hereby voided. Sellers are advised to seek legal advice."

The education available to agents is an advantage, although it is often designed to make you a better agent, not a better investor. If you do not have a license, don't get one unless you want to work as an agent and collect commissions.

If you already have a license and it does not have a negative impact on your investing, keep it until it does. Most sellers in a hurry would rather do business with someone in the business—someone who knows how to fill out a contract, someone who does not have to go to a bank and beg for money, someone who will really buy their house. Having a license is not a hindrance when you are buying from someone who really needs to sell.

14

BUYING AND SELLING HOUSES TO PRODUCE CASH FLOW—TODAY

Buying and selling a house for a quick profit is exciting work and can produce short-term cash flow. It is different from investing in a house; it takes more time and has more risk.

Buying and selling requires certain skills and takes a serious commitment of time. Many people who attempt this strategy are unsuccessful, because they underestimate the amount of skill and time it takes to buy and sell for a profit.

Buying and holding a house for a long-term profit requires less skill, because time is on your side. You can buy a house at a retail price, and if you hold it long enough, you will make a profit. The longer you hold a property in a good location, the more money you will make.

As an investor, you will acquire the skills you need as you research your area, talk to hundreds (yes, hundreds) of sellers, and negotiate and close deals.

When you have the needed skills, you can buy some houses for investment and others to increase your cash flow today. If you are trying to transition from working for someone else to being a full-time real estate investor, buying and selling a couple of houses a year can give you the cash you will need for down payments and living expenses.

If you are already a full-time investor, you are constantly looking for good deals. Sometimes you will find houses that you do not want to buy and rent. Rather than just passing on such a property, buy and sell it for a profit.

To qualify as a good long-term investment, a house should be well designed, well built, be in a neighborhood that will attract long-term tenants, and appreciate at an above-average rate. Most who buy to resell are less particular about which house and in which neighborhood they buy.

TIME IS YOUR FRIEND AS AN INVESTOR, BUT NOT WHEN YOU ARE BUYING AND SELLING

When you are buying and selling houses for short-term profit, time works against you. It may take you several months to find and buy a good deal. After you close on the deal, every day you own it the holding costs (interest, taxes, insurance, advertising, repairs) reduce your profit. To make a profit, you need to sell before your profits are eaten up by your holding costs.

Your annual profit from buying and selling houses depends on several factors:

1. How far below the market you buy each house
2. How many houses you are able to buy a year
3. How long it takes you to sell and close
4. How much you can sell for

Some investors buy multiple houses and wholesale them quickly to other investors, but make only a little on each house. Others buy just a few houses and sell at a retail price to make a larger profit per house.

ANNUAL PROFIT = PROFIT PER HOUSE × NUMBER OF HOUSES BOUGHT AND SOLD

The key to making a profit is buying a house at a below-market price and then reselling as quickly as possible. You cannot sell a house in a short time at an above-market price. The higher the price, the longer it will take to sell.

If you can find a house that you can buy 15 to 20 percent below the market in two months, close the purchase and fix it up in two months, and sell and close it in two more months (an optimistic time table), you are on track to buy and sell two houses a year. If your goal is to make $60,000 a year, you need to net $30,000 profit per house.

This can be a good business if you are a skilled buyer and able to invest time and energy to the work and able to buy below the market consistently. Many who buy to resell are not accomplished negotiators and buyers. They buy marginal deals and try to make a profit by selling at above-market prices.

You want to be good at buying and selling for more reasons than just making money. The more houses you buy and sell in a year, the more you have to work and the more risks you take. You want to be skillful enough and professional enough in your work to make your efforts worthwhile and insulate you from litigation.

Many legal issues arise and a good number of lawsuits result from buy/sell transactions that go awry. The other party (it could be either the buyer or the seller) feels as if she has been taken advantage of, or a flaw in the property surfaces after the closing. Sometimes these issues can only be resolved with a lawsuit, but a lawsuit can eat up years of profits.

FIVE STEPS TO MAKING MONEY BUYING AND SELLING HOUSES

1. *Identify the price range of houses in your town that sells the fastest.* You want to buy houses to resell in this price range. A Realtor can give you this information. Typically, it is a house you would call a starter house or one step above that house. It is often just below the median-priced house in a town. Often there is a large inventory of these houses, and although there is competition to buy, these houses are easier to sell.

   A cardinal rule of real estate is that it is easier to buy than to sell. When you are the buyer, you are in control. You can choose how much to offer and decide whether to buy or pass. When you are selling, you can lower your price and offer terms to attract buyers, but you cannot make them buy. You can lead a buyer to a good deal, but you can't make them buy.

2. *Identify several neighborhoods that have houses for sale in the price range you want to buy and sell.* Look for signs of opportunity, like the

opportunities listed in Chapter 4. An empty house, any house that is not well maintained, or a house with a bad tenant all signal opportunity.

Walk the streets in the neighborhoods that interest you and look carefully at each house on the street. You will notice houses that you would not see driving the street. Talk to the neighbors. Knock on doors and ask if they know of any houses in the neighborhood for sale. This is the most effective way to find a good deal. Good deals are rarely listed.

Most houses that are opportunities are not even for sale. There will be no sign in the yard and no ad in the paper. Many people in trouble simply hope that their problem will solve itself and take no action to solve it. This is why walking through a neighborhood and knocking on doors is such an effective way to find a good deal.

3. ***Once you find a good deal, research it.*** Find out what the owner paid and what others have paid for similar houses on the street recently.

4. ***Now set a minimum profit goal.*** A more expensive house that may be harder to resell should command a larger profit. Likewise, a house that needs considerable work and will consume a lot of your time and money needs to produce a larger profit.

   For a beginning buyer, a profit goal of 10 percent of the purchase price is a good ***minimum*** target. That is *net profit*, after repairs and holding costs

5. ***Start keeping a journal.*** Every time you buy a house, write down in your journal the following points:
   - Why you thought that this house would be a good deal
   - How you came up with your first offer
   - How the buyer responded to the offer
   - What the offer was that was accepted
   - What you would offer if you could start over

Before you make your next offer, review the last offer that you had accepted and try to make this next offer a little better for you. As you become more skilled, increase your profit-per-house goal. Experienced buyers command 20 percent or greater profits.

If you are willing to work for less than a 10 percent profit, get a real estate license and collect a commission. You don't have to take the risk, make a down payment, or pay the carrying costs that being in the buy/sell business requires. In the process of getting a license, you will learn the laws that regulate agents in your state. Hopefully, you will learn about contracts, deeds, closing statements, title insurance, and other facets of the real estate business.

If you intend to receive a 10 percent return on your money (and consider a return on your time as well), then you need to work on your skills and devote the time required to buy and sell houses for profit. The 10 and 20 percent figures are just profit targets. Anyone who actually has bought and sold a property will tell you that you don't always make as much as you plan to make. Sometimes you get lucky and make more, but it often takes longer to sell or costs more to make repairs than you planned, and your profit is less than your target.

A REALTOR WHO WORKED FOR LESS THAN A COMMISSION

A Realtor bought a house from me that needed updating. I had owned it for about ten years and had rented it to the same tenant for that entire time. The house had more than doubled in value, and the Realtor made me an offer I did not refuse.

She fixed it up and sold it several months later for about a $5,000 gross profit (not counting her holding costs or taxes). She would have made more money listing and selling it without spending the time and investing the money to fix it up and market it.

You can make more than $5,000 per house when you buy and sell, but there are no guarantees. Other investors have sold houses to me for less than they paid after trying unsuccessfully to sell for a profit.

A long-term investor can wait patiently for a strong market, keeping a house rented until the time is right to sell, and harvest a large profit. A short-term "flipper" does not have that luxury.

After you buy a house at a bargain price, you have to sell it for more than you paid for it, plus your holding costs, plus any money you have to invest to improve the house. Short-term profits you make from buying and selling are subject to the higher tax rates applied to ordinary income, not the capital gains rate available on investment property gains.

Taxes will become a greater concern once you begin to make a lot of money. Learn to make money first, and then learn how to reduce your taxes. If you are broke, you don't need a good tax strategy or asset-protection plan. You need assets and income.

Once your taxable income from buying and selling exceeds $30,000 a year, talk with a certified public accountant (CPA) who owns real estate himself about options that can reduce your tax liability. Using a corporation or limited-liability company (LLC) to buy and sell properties can reduce your tax bill and give you some liability protection. There are both advantages and disadvantages to using an entity to buy and sell, so get good advice before you spend the money to form one.

WHICH HOUSES TO BUY AND WHICH HOUSES NOT TO BUY

There are some houses you should not buy at any price. There are houses that are beyond repair at a reasonable cost (unless you are buying at below the lot value) and houses in neighborhoods where there are no owner occupants and no trend toward more owner occupants. When a neighborhood is entirely owned by landlords, your only buyers will be other landlords. You might be able to sell to them at a profit, but they will be tough negotiators, and often these pros will want you to finance the property.

The ideal house to buy is one in a neighborhood with many owner occupants who maintain their property, a neighborhood where buyers will want to live and will pay a retail price when they buy. A house that needs only carpet, paint, and minor repairs is safer to buy than one that needs a total rehab. The more work a house needs, the more money you will have to invest and the longer it will take you to make a profit. The more money you have invested, the more pressure you have to resell quickly. That often leads you to accept a lower offer than you planned.

SELLING HOUSES THAT NEED WORK IN "AS IS" CONDITION

CASE STUDY: THE HOUSE OF THE RISING WATER

I bought a house from a bank that had neglected to maintain it. The bank had allowed a roof to leak for months during the rainy season, and the water in the house was getting deeper by the week. The ceilings had fallen in, the kitchen cabinets had fallen off the walls, and all the drywall was soaked.

This house needed work!

I put together the following projection of the cost to buy and repair the house and then to sell it:

Purchase price:	$90,000
Estimated cost of repairs:	$50,000
Time to make repairs:	2 months
Time to market and close:	2 months
Estimated holding and marketing costs:	$5,000
Total projected investment:	$145,000
Estimate selling price:	$189,000
Projected profit before taxes:	$44,000

Once I had a contract to buy the house from the bank, I put a for sale sign in the yard. I had several calls, because many buyers are looking for bargains that need work. There was one family who wanted to buy the house but did not have enough money or credit to buy it; however, they did have the ability and resources to do the work needed. *Never sell a house that needs work to a buyer unless the buyer can convince you that he can do the work needed.*

I agreed to sell them the house on a one-year lease/option contract in "as is" condition with a $1,000 down payment at a price of $120,000. I gave the buyers three months' reduced rent ($100 a month) and had

(continued)

them agree in the written contract specifically what work they would do during that three months.

Their plan was to get the house in livable condition in the first three months. Working with friends from their church, they were able to clean out the house, repair it, move in, and get it financed at a bank with an appraisal of $189,000 within six months. They borrowed enough money to pay me in full and recover most of their expenses.

The results:

My purchase price:	$90,000
My cost of repairs:	$0
Time to market and close:	6 months
Actual holding costs:	$3,000
(I collected 3 months' rent)	
Total investment:	$93,000
Selling price:	$120,000
Profit before taxes:	$27,000

Although I made less money, I significantly reduced my risk and time invested. If the buyers had not closed on their contract, I would have owned a much better house than I turned over to them.

When you have a house that needs this much work, typically you go over budget on both time and money. When you can take an acceptable profit and let someone else take the responsibility for the work, you free up your time to look for the next good deal. You also eliminate or at least reduce your risk.

Selling a house with a small down payment has risks. If the house needs a lot of work and your buyers do some or all of that work, the work they contribute is the equivalent of a bigger down payment. If a house needs no work, require a larger cash down payment. If the sale falls through, you need enough cash to make any needed repairs to the house and remarket it.

15

SELLING ON LEASE/OPTIONS TO GENERATE LARGER PROFITS

To make a great buy, you typically have to sign a contract to buy the house today and then close within a few days. The reason people sell houses for far less than what they are worth is because they have to: they don't have enough time to wait for a retail buyer.

When you sell a house, if you sell to a buyer who cannot close right away—who needs some time to pay you—you can sell for a significantly higher price. I often make an additional $10,000 per house when I sell on a short-term lease/option contract.

In the case of the "house of the rising water," I sold the house using a lease/option contract. A lease/option is a form of owner financing, but a simpler, safer, and less costly way to sell to a buyer who may not be able to qualify for a loan.

Most buyers who want owner financing cannot qualify for a bank loan. There are always a substantial number of house buyers—or would-be buyers—who cannot qualify for a bank loan because of poor credit or low income. Some owner wannabes are eager to buy and are willing to pay a retail price and make regular payments if they are given the opportunity.

Using a lease/option, I sell many families their first home. They pay an option payment and then monthly lease payments for the term of the contract. If they want to buy the house, they must at some point qualify for a bank loan.

QUALIFIYING YOUR BUYERS

Before I sell to them, I get financial information and identify why they cannot qualify today for a loan. I help them to form a plan so that they can qualify within a period of time, often one or two years. If they have too many expenses, often the solution is to pay off a credit card debt or a car loan—and to avoid new debt. If they have poor credit because of overdue bills, I counsel them to form a plan to pay off those bills and then to begin making timely payments on their other credit accounts.

SETTING THE OPTION PAYMENT, THE RENT, AND THE PRICE

The option payment, the monthly rental amount, and the price you'll sell the house for are directly related. You can charge a higher sales price if you will accept a lower option payment and rent. However, if no one ever buys because your price is too high, then you will never sell the house.

Which of the three—option payment, rent, or price—has the greatest impact on your total profit? If you increase the option payment from $3,000 to $5,000, how does that affect your profit? If the optionee doesn't buy, you get to keep a larger option payment, but if the optionee does buy, you make the same amount of profit.

Raising the monthly rent will produce more income, but you must balance the amount of rent you charge with how long it will take you to rent the house. If you try to get an extra $100 a month, and the house sits empty for a month, you probably have lost more than you can recover. Using a lower rent and renting faster often will make you more money.

Of the three variables, the price is the one that will have the greatest impact on your profit. If you make someone a good deal on the rent and accept a relatively small option deposit, but set your price at the top of the retail range, you will collect several thousands of dollars more in profit when you close.

GETTING THE BEST PRICE WHEN YOU SELL

Table 15.1 presents an example of what you may be able to charge for a house in a typical market, one appreciating from 3 to 6 percent. Notice that both the price and rent are expressed in ranges. It is impossible to put an exact price or rent on a house. If you had four appraisers give you a price, you would get four different prices. You need to know your market well enough that you can establish these ranges. Establish a range for both price and rent that allows you to form a strategy for selling.

Selling on lease/options is an art, not a science. Every house will have a different market appeal: Some will need lots of work, and others will be ready to move into. The desirability of the neighborhood will determine how many people will want the house and how much they are willing to pay. Table 15.1 shows the relationship between what price you ask, what rent you ask, and the amount of option money you are able to command.

Notice which number has the greatest impact on your profit—it's the price. By charging a lower rent and deposit, you can charge a higher price. The amount of the deposit you charge will have an impact on the number of buyers who actually close. The lower the deposit you charge, the fewer the number of buyers who will be able to close on the purchase.

TABLE 15.1 A Bargain Rent and Option Payment
Produce a Higher Price and Greater Profit

Today's retail house value:	$240,000–$260,000	
Today's market rent:	$1,500–$1,750	
Market condition:	Prices Appreciating 3%–6%	

Price	Option Payment	Rent
$230,000	$10,000	$1,800
$240,000	$7,500	$1,700
$250,000	$6,000	$1,600
$260,000	$5,000	$1,500
$270,000	$4,000	$1,400

A buyer with more money and better credit is likely to be a better negotiator and often will negotiate the sales price. If you can sell at a higher price and still collect a larger down payment, do it. It is probably a sign that the market is heating up and that prices will be moving up faster.

The time it takes you to sell the house will be determined by how you price it. If you ask for a high price, high rent, and a high deposit, it may take you months to sell. In an average market, you can sell a house on a lease/option in a month or less if you price it at retail and charge a fair rent and deposit.

If getting a higher price is more important to you than getting more rent or more money up front, then you should advertise the house with a lower down payment and rent to make it more attractive to more buyers.

If getting your money sooner is more important to you, then selling at a lower price and getting a larger deposit will increase the chance of the buyers actually closing. The more they have invested up front, the harder they will work to close on the house.

The option payment is part of the money you are asking for before you give a lease/option buyer possession of the house. You also will collect the first month's rent—in cash. The total amount you collect needs to be low enough to attract buyers. The condition of the house and the desirability of the house will determine how much you can charge.

My student Bob Bruss advised to advertise the amount of money it takes to move you in:

Lease/option: $5,000 moves you in

Quaint 3/2/2 on quiet street: $399,000

Call Bob at 222-222-2222

Bob invested in the San Francisco area and sold houses in high price ranges on lease/options with relatively small down payments.

DON'T USE LEASE/OPTIONS AS A MANAGEMENT TOOL

Some lease/option sellers never actually sell a house. They sign a lease/option to renters who could never qualify for a loan. These sellers are just collecting additional money in the form of option payments every time they rent the property.

Use a lease/option to sell a house that you want to sell. Don't use it as a technique to increase your cash flow from your long-term investments. There are risks to selling your investment houses on lease/options. First, if the market takes off and prices jump 15 to 20 percent in one year, many of your buyers will buy. This will take you out of the market just when you want to own property.

Suppose that you owned ten houses and instead of renting them, you sold them all on lease/options to increase your cash flow and reduce your maintenance costs. (Later, in Chapter 17, you will learn how to rent to tenants who will take care of your property.)

House prices jump 20 percent, and eight of ten of your tenants buy their houses, leaving you with a large tax bill to pay or the challenge of reinvesting your money in property in a market that's going up 20 percent a year. If the houses were worth an average of $200,000, you have given up (20% × $200,000) or about $40,000 per house profit.

The lease/option is the best way to sell a property at a retail price, but don't make the mistake of selling property that you want to keep. When you buy a house in a strong neighborhood with good long-term financing, don't sell it just because someone wants to buy it. Your best houses will make you the most money. Others constantly will try to buy them from you.

SETTING THE TERM, MONTHLY CREDIT, AND EXTENSIONS

When you sell a house, use a one-year lease/option period. If house prices jump 10 percent during the year, you are giving less away when you use a short term. If the buyers are nervous (and they often are) that one year may not be enough time for them to solve the problem that keeps them from qualifying for a loan, then offer them a one-year extension—at a higher price. In an average market, use a 5 percent increase in both the price and the rent for the second year. If the market is increasing at a faster rate, ask for a larger increase. You can always give some of the increase back if you want to sell the house and it does not appraise at the higher price when the buyers apply for a loan.

Put in your lease/option agreement a monthly credit amount toward the purchase that the buyers will "receive" when they pay on time. Use $100 a month. If you use a higher amount, the lender who the buyers borrow from may disallow it unless they are paying a credit on top of the fair market rent. While a larger credit may make the buyers more interested in buying the house, it will not help them to get a loan. If they accumulate a large credit and then cannot buy the house, they may feel entitled to part of it if they cannot buy.

BEING A GOOD GUY IF THEY CANNOT BUY

Reporters have asked me what percentage of my lease/option buyers actually close. Overall, it's about 50 percent, but it depends on the credit market. When interest rates are low and loans are easier to come by, the percentage of buyers who can qualify for a loan and close goes way up—to 100 percent in some years. When interest rates rise and loans are hard to get unless you have perfect credit, then the percentage of buyers drops.

When that happens, I often renegotiate the agreement so that the buyers can stay in the house and continue to try to buy it. I adjust the rent and price to keep up with the market. Eventually, if the buyers clean up their credit, they can buy the house.

In the event that the buyers change their mind, get transferred, or get divorced, sick, or any of the real-world things that happen to people every day, then I offer some of their original deposit back if they have paid the rent and taken care of the property. In effect, I treat them like a good tenant and refund part of their original option money, treating it like a security deposit.

This is a nice thing to do, and it is also good business. If you have to go through the eviction process to move out a tenant who was buying under a lease/option, it will cost you both your time and money. It is better business to give the buyers some of their own money back as an incentive to move and give you back a house in good condition than to use the courts to force them out.

If you get a house back in good condition, then you can resell it quickly to another lease/option tenant.

GETTING YOUR CASH NOW WHEN YOU SELL ON LEASE/OPTIONS

When you buy a house that you intend to sell on a lease/option, you may need to recover part of the cash that you have tied up in the house before the buyers close on their lease/option contract. A bank line of credit and a private line of credit are good ways to obtain the cash you need before you receive your profit.

Suppose that you bought and sold this house:

Market value today:	$170,000 to $180,000
Your purchase price:	$150,000
Your down payment:	$30,000
Your loan:	$120,000

You resell on a lease/option:

Sale price:	$179,900
Option payment:	$5,000
Balance due:	$174,900
Your loan balance:	$120,000 (This will be adjusted at closing to include any monthly credits the buyers have earned.)
Your equity in the contract:	$54,900

You now have about $55,000 of equity in the contract and about $25,000 cash tied up in the house (your $30,000 down payment less the $5,000 down payment). You can use this contract to borrow $25,000 on a short-term loan either from a bank or from a private party. You can show the lender that she will be repaid from the proceeds at the closing. You could assign your contract as collateral for the loan if she insists, but often you can borrow unsecured.

If the house does not close as planned, you will sell it again and pay off your loan when it does close.

If you are getting the money from a private investor, you could sell her a half interest in your equity in the house, subject to the lease/option sale, for $25,000. The investor would then own one-half the house and would receive one-half the rent as well as the proceeds ($54,900/2 = $27,450) when the sale closes. If the first sale does not close, then you would resell the house at hopefully a higher price, and the investor would then participate in half that sale.

A BUSINESS PLAN FOR BUYING AND SELLING

If you want to make buying and selling a full-time business, you need a plan to produce a certain amount of income. Here is a simple plan that you can use as a format to form your own plan. Plug in real numbers in your town to see how it would work for you.

Annual income goal:	$80,000
Price range of houses that will sell quickly:	$140,000 to $150,000
Projected average profit per house (year one):	$20,000
Number of houses needed to meet income goal:	4
Average down payment required to buy a house:	$20,000
Average option payment received when selling:	$5,000
Cash needed to buy first house:	$20,000

Borrowing against the first contract could raise the down payment for the second house. With $80,000 in initial capital, you could acquire all four houses without borrowing.

Compare this business with other small businesses that you could own and operate in your town. Most small businesses require far more than $80,000 in startup capital. They also require employees, and have overhead such as rent, advertising, utilities, and so on. Many businesses have inventory that can spoil (like food), go out of style (like shoes), or be stolen. Your inventory is appreciating, won't go out of style, and it's hard to steal.

The owner of a small business often works or is on call many hours, seven days a week; in addition to his own work, such an owner must supervise the work of his employees. You alone, working part-time, can generate more net income than most small businesses in your town.

DOING GOOD WORK AND GETTING PAID FOR IT

The business of buying and selling houses provides a service to your community. There are always sellers who need to sell quickly and buyers with credit problems who need help buying. By treating people fairly and by filling both these needs, you can make a good living *and* help people out of difficult situations. At the same time, you can hold on to the better properties for long-term investment, which will one day give you the ability to simply collect rent rather than continue to buy and sell.

When you sell on a lease/option, you can have the buyers pay your closing costs, and you sell the house in its "as is" condition.

How Much Does Selling on Lease/Option Save You?

Here is a comparison of a lease/option sale and a sale through an agent:

Market value of house: $150,000 to $160,000   Rent: $1,200

	Through Realtor	With Lease /Option
Offering price:	$159,950	$159,950
Sale price:	$155,000	$159,950
Commission:	$10,850	$0
Closing costs:	$1,200	$0
Net proceeds:	$142,950	$159,950
Date you receive the money:	90 to 180 days	1 year+
Rent received during the year:	$0	$14,400

The advantages of selling through a professional agent are that you are sometimes paid sooner and you do not have to talk and show to potential buyers, and then close the deal. Not all houses listed for sale sell during the first listing period. You might have to wait the best part of a year to be paid, even selling through a good agent.

Every day you wait you are supporting an empty house. This often puts so much pressure on a seller that they sell the house for far less than what it is worth. Agents will put pressure on you to reduce your price if the house does not sell quickly. No sale means no commission to them. A low price increases the chances of a sale. It's good for them but costly to you.

With a lease/option, you collect rent while you wait for the house to close. If it takes a year, you collect the rent each month while you wait. This results in a higher net profit to you.

Selling to a Family Member Using a Lease/Option

You may have a family member who is interested in investing but who is short of funds. You could sell that person a house that you want to sell using a lease/option. You could make them a good deal on both the rent and the price to give that person a better than average chance of making a profit. You could even help the person manage the property and provide a little advice along the way.

When selling to a family member, you could use a longer-term lease/option to give the person more time to make a profit. You might plan for your relative to refinance and pay you off when the property increases 50 percent in value. If in your town that would take about five years, you could use that term and then renegotiate if the person needed more time.

Should it not work out, then you would still own the house. It is better to sell to a family member using a lease/option for a couple of reasons:

1. You don't have to report the sale on your tax return until the relative exercises the option to buy. If he doesn't buy, you still own it and have not had to report a sale.
2. You don't have to foreclose to recover title to the property. You would not want to foreclose on a family member.

SELLING TO ANOTHER INVESTOR USING A LEASE/OPTION

If you have no one in your family who wants to invest, there are many young investors getting started today who would eagerly buy from you on a lease/option. You could sell at a retail price without a commission. The investor then would manage the property and pay you when she resold it or refinanced it.

16

FINDING AND BUYING PREFORECLOSURES AND FORECLOSURES

Buying property from an owner in distress is exciting and can be very profitable. However, it is often complicated and requires specialized knowledge of the system and the law.

If you are a beginning investor, read this chapter, but know that you need some experience before you have success buying foreclosures. When you find an opportunity, use a competent real estate attorney who can guide you through the process of buying your first foreclosure. Another investor may be able to refer you to a knowledgeable attorney.

HOW AND WHY FORECLOSURES OCCUR

It is easy to borrow money against a home you own. Sometimes it is too easy, and homeowners borrow more than they can afford to repay. When this happens and the borrower stops making payments, both the lender and the homeowner have a problem.

Most lenders do not want to foreclose a loan and take title to a property. They are not property managers; they are lenders. Often, when they foreclose, they lose money on the loan. They cannot sell the property for enough to recover the loan balance and cost.

When a borrower loses a house in foreclosure, the event has a long-lasting effect on the borrower's credit. When the borrower is able to borrow money again, it will be at a much higher interest rate. Banks will be reluctant to make another home loan to that borrower for many years.

Even more distressing is loss of the family home and the need to move abruptly into less of a house in a weaker neighborhood. This is traumatic to a family and can cause other family problems. If you can offer a solution to this serious financial problem, you can save the homeowner a lot of grief and money and personally make a substantial profit for your skill and efforts.

Foreclosures can result from misfortune, such as an accident, illness, or a job layoff. More often they are a result of a homeowner borrowing money on terms he cannot afford. Regardless of the reason for the foreclosure, the key to buying a property from an owner facing foreclosure is how you deal with the owner and the problem.

BEWARE OF THE FORECLOSURE SHARKS

Some people who buy properties in foreclosure are not tactful or even ethical. Buyers who use high-pressure tactics to get sellers who are behind in their payments to sign a contact may be breaking the law. Buyers who "steal" property, leaving nothing on the table for the sellers, don't get many referrals or make many friends.

BUYING FORECLOSURES AND MAKING FRIENDS WHILE DOING IT

There is a different approach to buying properties in foreclosure. Much of my business comes from referrals. Previous sellers, borrowers, buyers, renters, and agents call me with repeat business and send me their friends. You can buy property from owners in distress and leave them with their honor intact and happy that they did business with you. The secret: deal with others as you would like to be treated if you were in their situation, and solve the problem.

NOT ALL FORECLOSURES ARE OPPORTUNITIES

Some property in foreclosure—as with property in general—is not worth buying because of its bad location or poor condition. Some owners are just too difficult to help or to make a deal with. Do not stray from your investment plan just to buy a property in foreclosure. Only look at houses in price ranges and in neighborhoods that you understand and that you know are profitable.

Often properties are in foreclosure because of a bad location, bad design, or bad concept. These problems may be expensive or even impossible to fix. If you buy these properties, even at a bargain price, you may become the next owner in distress. Frequently you will see the same house foreclosed on several times—there is a problem with that house, not just the owners.

FIVE SOURCES OF DELINQUENT HOMEOWNERS WHO NEED YOU

1. Homeowners who are in trouble and still trying to borrow more money

When a homeowner falls behind on her first mortgage, she often will try to borrow more against the house from a second mortgage lender to catch up on the payments on the first. These second mortgages are recorded in the public records and can be a source of leads.

Some lenders are much more aggressive than others and will make higher-risk loans. While most lenders want a certain level of credit and income, some lenders will loan to nearly anyone with income, even if that person is behind on his first loan and jobless.

Learn who the most aggressive lenders are in your area, and recognize that only the most desperate borrowers will borrow from them. Their interest rates and up-front fees will be high—and so will their default rate. If these borrowers were in financial trouble before, borrowing more money at a high interest rate will only compound their trouble. When you identify these borrowers, you are identifying people who may need to sell their house soon—and in a hurry.

You can identify these borrowers by searching the public records for loans recorded by these high-risk lenders and then contacting the borrowers. Simply tell them that you are looking for a house in their neighborhood, and ask them if they know anyone who wants to sell. This low-key approach opens the door to asking more questions if they admit that they want to sell.

Another direct approach is to meet with the people making these loans. They are paid on commission when they make a loan. You can offer them a finder's fee to refer homeowners to you who need to sell, not borrow more. Even the most aggressive lenders turn down some homeowners because they have too much debt already. These homeowners may have little equity, but the lenders they owe may be willing to renegotiate the terms of their loans, allowing you to buy for a profit.

2. A second source of owners in trouble is advertising, bandit signs, and mailing postcards

Cash for Your House
Fast Closing
Save Your Equity
Call John anytime at 222-222-2222

Another approach that gets calls is:
Private Investor Has Cash
for Notes and Mortgages
Call John anytime at 222-222-2222

Ads and signs will get calls from people looking to sell or needing a loan. Both will generate leads. Your challenge will be screening them and following up on the good leads. Use a phone number that you can answer often; many of these people will not leave a callback number. If your regional newspaper is too expensive to run an ad for a month, try one of your small papers or shoppers.

Mailing postcards can be effective, but targeting your mail to those who might be in trouble means compiling or buying a qualified list. It will take repeated mailings to the same owners to get a response. I have seen stacks of letters and postcards from foreclosure buyers in houses that I have purchased. It's a competitive and expensive way to find opportunity.

3. A third source is other house buyers who will be your "bird dog"

If your town is like mine, you have bandit signs or ads that say "I will buy your house for cash." If you own houses, you may be getting letters from these same people. The buyers with these signs have limited cash. I have found that every buyer seems to have a favorite type of house and a favorite neighborhood. The secret is to find another buyer who is short on cash or has an interest different from yours and offer to pay him for leads on the houses that you like. These "bird dogs" will find you opportunities for a small fee, typically a few thousand dollars.

4. A fourth source is referrals from bankers and other lenders whom you may know

Local lenders often refer troubled homeowners to other lenders; when such homeowners are in too much trouble to borrow more, they refer them to buyers.

Understand that lenders will not call you and tell you about their customer. They will call their customers and tell them about you. To get these referrals, the lender must first know that you buy houses and then trust that you will treat people fairly. Lenders do not want negative repercussions from referring business to you.

5. A fifth source is property in good neighborhoods that is being neglected

I frequently drive and walk through neighborhoods I like, looking for empty or physically distressed property. While not every property that needs work is an opportunity, it is a free phone call to the owners to find out if they want to sell. Even if you only buy one in a hundred and it takes you three months to find one that you can buy, this is highly profitable work.

There are more sources, but this is enough to get you started. *The key is you.* You need to do research, make contacts, run ads, and canvas neighborhoods to generate the leads that you need. There are always opportunities.

TALKING WITH OWNERS IN FORECLOSURE

Many owners in foreclosure are not willing to answer questions or even admit that they have a problem. Try to help them, but don't spend too much time with them unless they admit to needing help and are willing to accept it.

Explain the consequences of a foreclosure:

1. Poor credit will cause them to pay higher interest rates.
2. They may have to move into a much less desirable house.
3. They may not have enough money to move into any house.
4. They will lose their equity.
5. A new job or a promotion may require a credit check. An applicant who is under severe financial stress may not be a desirable employee.
6. A foreclosure can be a long-term family disaster.

TESTING THE OWNER'S MOTIVATION

Most sellers want you to come to look at their house. As a test of their motivation and willingness to cooperate, ask a homeowner in distress to come to you. Ask her to bring all her paperwork on the house.

Specifically ask for loan documents, title insurance, closing documents from the purchase, and any refinancing and all correspondence from the lender or lenders. These documents will give you the information you need to assess the situation and consider if you are part of a solution. A solution would be to make the owner an offer if you can make a profit in a transaction that solves her problem.

GIVING SOUND ADVICE TO DELINQUENT BORROWERS

Borrowing more money is not a solution when you cannot make your current payments. Unless you can roll the back payments into a new loan with a lower payment, you are just getting deeper into trouble. Refinancing loans in default is expensive and often has high closing costs and high interest rates. It may buy a little time, but often at a high cost.

If the house has enough equity to refinance, it has enough equity to sell. Selling may net the owners some cash, avoid a foreclosure, and give the owners some options they would not have if they were foreclosed.

Never lend money to anyone behind on his payments. First, it is not good for them. If they cannot make their payments now, how could they make new, higher payments? Second, there are complex laws in many states that protect homeowners who are in default from unscrupulous lenders. You may violate one of those laws even when you are trying to help.

BUYING A HOUSE FROM AN OWNER IN DEFAULT

Buying homes from owners in foreclosure is not as simple as it seems on late-night TV. Your first challenge is finding owners (1) who are behind in their payments, (2) who own a house that you want, and (3) who will agree to sell. Finding them is not difficult; getting them to make a good decision (to sell to you) can be. They did not get into financial trouble by making good decisions.

Another challenge is dealing with the lenders. In this era of megabanks, it's a challenge to find the right person to talk to. Many loans in default are owed to lenders who have made higher-risk second mortgage loans. These lenders often are eager to talk because they are in a risky position. Some of these lenders are private individuals who are just trying to recover their capital.

A third challenge is finding the money to fund these purchases. Foreclosure buying can require a lot of cash. Lenders often will want cash for their positions. Investors who will loan you money at decent rates and will co-invest in longer-term deals are a good source, along with home equity loans and lines of credit.

DEALING WITH THE LENDERS

When borrowers quit making their loan payments, the lender begins writing letters trying to inspire them to pay. Understand that lenders do not want the real estate. They want their money back. While some lenders do make a profit when they foreclose, many more lose money. Foreclosures are an expensive distraction from their main source of profits—lending money.

A junior lender, one who has made a second, third, or even fourth position (behind other loans), is taking a bigger risk and often will be more aggressive and more creative in collecting her money.

Many first mortgages are insured for nonpayment through the Federal Housing Administration (FHA) or Mortgage Guarantee Insurance Corporation (MGIC) or are guaranteed by the Veterans Administration (VA), so the lender's risk is lower. Second mortgage lenders rarely have insurance, so they are more willing to accept a partial payment when a loan is in default.

SOLVING THE DELINQUENT OWNER'S BIGGEST PROBLEM

To homeowners facing foreclosure, ruined credit and loss of equity are both small problems compared with having to move their family out of their home. They are facing a move into a rental house in a neighborhood that probably is far less desirable than their current one. An owner who has to move because of a foreclosure is no catch as a tenant and may have to accept the dregs of the rental market. Obviously, if an owner did not pay the lender, he may not pay the rent either.

You can solve this one big problem, but you must solve it carefully or you can become the victim. If you buy a house in foreclosure and then rent it back to the owners, there are three requirements:

1. Make sure that the sellers understand what they are doing. Because they are not moving, they may think that they are borrowing money, not selling their home. Be clear in what you say and specific in what you write down. Document clearly that this is a sale, not a loan. In a separate document, agree to rent the former owners the house.

2. Something has to change before renting to the sellers makes sense (either the house they are in or another rental you have). Has their income increased or their expenses decreased? How much rent can they afford to pay? They proved that they cannot afford the current house payments. How much can they afford?

3. Always build in a financial incentive for the sellers to pay the rent on time and then at some point to move out of the house and leave it in good condition. You want them to be able to afford the rent and then to leave you a house in good condition when they leave. They will be more likely to do these things if they are paid to do them. Build into your offer a below market rent if they pay on time, and also more money in the form of a large security deposit when they move out, if they leave the house clean and in good repair.

Buying a House and Renting It Back to an Owner Who Is Behind on His Payments

Many homeowners who are behind on their payments like their house and don't want to move. Moving is expensive and not a lot of fun. You can buy a house using this strategy, but you must use a great deal of caution and common sense. Remember: If the homeowner is not making payments to the lender, you have to structure a deal that she can afford, or she won't make payments to you either.

Important Note: Some states have laws designed to protect sellers who are behind in their payments. These laws may address buying a house from a seller who is behind in his payments and then renting it back to him. Other states allow the seller to back out of the contract within a certain period of time. Understand your state laws that deal with foreclosures before entering into any agreement with sellers who are behind in their payments.

NEGOTIATING A PURCHASE AND LEASE

If the sellers have equity in their house, you can let them use that equity to pay rent on either their own house or another. For example, if their house is worth between $180,000 and $200,000 (always give yourself a range of prices) and their loan balance with back payments is $120,000, then they have enough equity that you can buy and give them bargain rent.

Retail value of house, clean and in good condition:	$180,000 to $200,000
Wholesale value of house in foreclosure:	$140,000 to $160,000
Balance on loan (including back payments and costs):	$120,000
Their equity:	$20,000

The owners' payments today (that they *cannot* afford) with taxes and insurance are $1,250 a month.

During your initial conversation, ask the owners what their house would rent for. They often have a high opinion of what their house is worth and what it will rent for. If during your negotiation you determine that they want to stay in their house, you can then use their rent estimate as a starting point.

If they guessed low or you are uncertain of the market rent, then you need to gather comparable market rent information to establish a rent. In the preceding example of a house with a wholesale value of $140,000, the market rent may be between $1,200 and $1,400 a month.

Next, it is important to determine the amount of rent that the owners can comfortably afford to pay. Ask them what they can afford. Ask them how much income they have. They should pay around one-third of their income in rent. Do not rent them the house at a rent higher than one-third of their income.

Next, establish the amount of security deposit that gives them enough incentive to give you the house in good condition. The amount will depend on the value and condition of the house and the risk that you are taking by renting them the house.

Always make the deposit greater than a month's rent. If the house is in good condition, use several months' rent. Some states have laws that set a maximum security deposit. Learn your state law—it will be under the "Landlord-Tenant" heading in your state statutes.

By keeping the rent low and the deposit high, you give the owners a large financial incentive to stay in the house and to give it back in good condition. If they leave early, you can rent the house to another tenant for more rent.

Assume that the owners in this example had lost their jobs but have now found new, lower-paying, jobs. Their monthly income has dropped from $5,000 to $3,000. With this income, they can afford to pay about 33 percent, or about $1,000 a month in rent.

Their greatest problem is finding affordable housing until they can get back on their feet. Moving is expensive. If you let them rent back their own home, you have saved them a lot of hard work and expense, not to mention the trauma of moving from their nice home into a neighborhood that they can currently afford.

Offer to rent them the house for one year at the bargain price of $900 a month, a $500 monthly discount from the high end of the market rent of $1,400. Understand that $1,400 is retail rent. If you rented to another tenant today, you would be more likely to collect around $1,300 a month.

Fair market rent:	$1,400
Rent to the previous owner:	$900
Monthly saving to them:	$500

If you rent to them for twelve months at this $500 discount, they would save $6,000. In addition, you could give them a credit of $4,000 as the security deposit, which you would refund at the end of the twelve months if they turn over the house clean and in good condition. Giving this large a credit as a security deposit is important. You need to give them a significant incentive to keep the house in good condition, leave it clean, and leave on time.

Calculating the benefit of the lease to them is as follows:

Discounted rent (12 months × $500):	$6,000
Security deposit:	$4,000
Total benefit if they stay 12 months:	$10,000

If they want to extend the lease and continue living in the house as tenants, then you can raise the rent to closer to a market rate. I have rented back to sellers for as long as five years at a reduced rate. You can build in an increase each year.

Using the preceding house with a market rent of between $1,200 and $1,400 today, a five-year monthly rent schedule could look like this:

Year one:	$900
Year two:	$1,200
Year three:	$1,300
Year four:	$1,400
Year five:	$1,500

By the time you reach the fifth year, you may be at market rent. Having a tenant stay in the house five years eliminates all vacancy costs, advertising costs, and a lot of maintenance expense. It can be a good deal for both you and the tenant. When you purchase a house using this technique, you often can make a deal that other buyers cannot make. You are offering a solution to the homeowners' biggest problem: where to live. In addition, you are saving them from a foreclosure, helping their credit.

Before you make the offer, calculate your potential profit, and make sure that the profit you will make will be fair for the amount of money and risk you are taking. In the preceding example, you are buying a house worth at least $140,000 for a total price of $130,000 (the loan balance of $120,000, the rent loss of $6,000, and the security deposit of $4,000). You may be able to buy this house with little or no down payment, depending on your ability to negotiate with the lender. If so, your risk is relatively low, and your profit potential when the former owners move out in a year should be a minimum of $10,000 and hopefully more.

Market value of house:	$180,000 to $200,000
Existing loan balance:	$120,000
Loss on rent ($350 × 12 months):	$4,200 ($1,250 loan payments less $900 rent)
Security deposit:	$4,000
Total:	$128,200
Your purchase price:	$128,200
Potential profit:	$50,000+

WHEN NEGOTIATING WITH LENDERS, ASK FOR MORE THAN YOU EXPECT

Before you take title to a property, contact the lender. You need to talk with a high-ranking employee who has the authority to renegotiate the terms of the loan. This may be the president of a small bank, the senior mortgage officer of a midsize bank, or the person in charge of the department in a large bank that handles delinquent loans. You often can get the name and number of the appropriate person from correspondence sent to the homeowners by the lender after they fall behind in their payments.

You often will begin with a lower-level employee and have to ask to speak with the supervisor. Keep asking until you get to a decision maker.

Remember, you are dealing with employees in a big institution. It's not their money, but a bad loan is their problem. You can be the solution to that problem.

If the lender is a community bank, go right to the president. She will be the decision maker and it is likely that some of what's owed *is* her money.

Once you are speaking to the right person, you need to have a plan. You can ask for many things that would benefit you, for example, a lower interest rate, a lower monthly payment, and the forgiveness of the back payments and penalties. If they won't forgive the back payments and penalties, ask them to add the amount of any delinquent payments to the loan. Often you can negotiate that the bank will let you sell the house to a new buyer who can assume the loan without qualifying.

Ask for a lot. It will work in your favor because the lender will see you as a professional buyer, not an amateur.

OFFER TO BANK WHEN BUYING A SECOND IN DEFAULT

If an institution owns the second mortgage or trust deed in default, see if it would be willing to lend you enough to pay off the first loan and add it to the second mortgage. That lender then would have a first mortgage in the amount of both the first and second mortgages.

House value:	$200,000
Second mortgage in default:	$50,000
Existing first mortgage:	$100,000

The bank with the second agrees to make a new first loan in the amount of $150,000 that would replace both existing loans.

Negotiate aggressively on the interest rate and terms so you will have cash flow immediately from the rents that you collect. You may agree to a shorter-term loan, say, ten years, to get a lower rate. If you need money to fix up or remodel the house, ask the lender to lend it to you and add it to the loan. If it's a great deal for you, but the lender is unwilling, offer to pay down the existing loan by $10,000. You could also give the lender a second mortgage on another house that you own with more equity.

BUYING AT A FORECLOSURE AUCTION

This is the most dangerous, but potentially lucrative, time to buy a property. Both lenders auctions and municipal auctions to collect back taxes are opportunities to buy at steep discounts, but the terms are all cash, often due the day of the sale, and you might not have much information about the property.

A house sold at a tax or foreclosure auction may be occupied. If owners are losing their home, or a tenant losing his rental, whoever is about to be evicted will not be happy. I've seen houses significantly destroyed by owners losing them. Tenants are unlikely to clean and paint on their way out, since they will not be getting their deposit back. It can take more money to repair the house than it is worth.

If you ever bid on a house in foreclosure, meet the occupants and offer to pay them to leave the house in good condition if you buy it. If you can agree on a reasonable number and you are the winning bidder at the sale, then you might get the house in good condition.

If you are not the winning bidder, find out who is and go talk with them. They may be willing to sell to you for a quick profit and you might be able to buy the house at a price that you like.

An empty house is much safer to buy. Just because it is empty today, is no guarantee that someone won't move in tonight. Empty houses in foreclosure often attract squatters, who will not improve the house.

BUYING FROM A LENDER THAT HAS FORECLOSED

A much safer time to buy is after the bank has foreclosed, evicted the occupants, and taken possession. The house may need a lot of work, but you have a good idea of how much. I have bought several bank-owned properties that were in good condition. That is the best house to buy, because you can rent it immediately.

Banks will often get multiple offers on REO (real estate owned) property. You increase your chances of buying by: (1) Offering all cash and a fast closing. Generally, ten days is acceptable. (2) Offer to accept the property in its "as is" condition, subject to your inspection. Your inspection period can run up to the date of closing if it's only ten days.

Banks can and do finance the sale of their foreclosures, but if the price is more important make a cash offer. See Chapter 8 for ideas on financing.

BUYING FORECLOSURES TAKES KNOWLEDGE AND EXPERIENCE

There are a lot of highly skilled, professional foreclosure buyers. This group includes attorneys and others with knowledge of the system and the market.

They are your competition. Buying foreclosures successfully requires experience, knowledge, and good legal advice.

In a rising interest-rate market, there are generally more foreclosures and a good deal of opportunity. Although tremendous opportunities are available, be careful not to buy beyond your ability to manage and handle the cash flow.

Let this be the beginning of your education, because there is much more to learn. If you are a beginning investor, get good legal advice before bidding at a foreclosure sale or entering into a contract to buy a property from owners who are behind on their payments. The laws that govern the sale of foreclosures change. Check them before you buy.

17

ATTRACTING AND TRAINING LONG-TERM, LOW-MAINTENANCE TENANTS

What qualities are you looking for in a good tenant? When I ask investors in my seminar this question, here are the responses I get:

1. A tenant who pays on time
2. A tenant who takes care of the property
3. A tenant who stays forever
4. A tenant who never calls

Now turn the question around. What is a good tenant (one who will do the preceding) looking for in a house and in a landlord? You probably have rented a house or an apartment. What was important to you as a renter? Here is a partial list of what good tenants tell me they are looking for:

1. A house in a safe neighborhood
2. A house big enough to hold all our stuff
3. A house that is clean and in good repair
4. A landlord who will maintain the property
5. Fair rent
6. Fair rent raises

7. Privacy
8. A house that is not for sale

Is there anything on this list that you would find difficult to provide?

THE SECRET OF GETTING THE BEST TENANTS IN YOUR TOWN

The best tenants have their choice of houses to rent, because every landlord with a vacancy would love to meet them. The secret to attracting the best tenants in your town is simple. Most of the features listed here were covered in Chapter 2. This is no accident: Buy a house that will attract a superior tenant.

Buy a well-designed house in a good neighborhood. Good neighbors are what everyone wants, and tenants are no exception. If the neighbors on both sides and across the street take good care of their property and are good neighbors, then you can attract a tenant who values a good neighbor.

Avoid neighborhoods full of tenants. Most landlords do not maintain property well or manage tenants well, so you can spot the tenant-occupied houses. Buy in owner-occupied neighborhoods, and then keep your house looking as good as the neighbors' houses.

Avoid houses with strange layouts. Some houses have been remodeled poorly, so you have to walk through one bedroom to get to another bedroom. These houses are hard to rent and hard to sell. Use your common sense to avoid houses that do not have a standard layout. You can buy them cheap, but in the long run, you will make less money.

Avoid houses on busy streets and on corner lots, and buy the best location you can afford. The best-located houses will appreciate the most and be easiest to rent.

BUY A HOUSE WITH ROOM FOR LOTS OF STUFF

Buy a house that is big enough for a family of four or five people to live in comfortably. Smaller families still appreciate the extra space, and it gives them room for guests or "new additions."

Houses with three bedrooms and two bathrooms and a garage or a basement are more rentable than a smaller home. You want to rent to a tenant who owns a bunch of stuff and does not find moving fun.

A yard that is fenced or that can be fenced is a great asset. Most of my tenants have kids or pets or both. One reason they need a house instead of an apartment is the kids and pets. Kids and pets increase the chances that the renters will stay a long time.

UNDERSTANDING THE LAWS
THAT APPLY TO LANDLORDING

There are local, state, and federal laws that affect you as a landlord. Your local laws, such as zoning regulations, determine what you can do with a property. A house zoned single-family residential may not be used to house a business. Other local laws may require you to maintain your property. Local code-enforcement departments generally enforce these laws.

Your state has laws that regulate the relationships between landlords and tenants. Get a copy of your state's landlord-tenant statute that applies to single-family rentals. Your state statutes will be available in your public library, and now they are often available online. It is almost certain that there are separate statute sections that apply to multifamily, mobile home, and commercial rentals.

Read the part of the law that deals with single-family tenancies carefully. Learn what maintenance you are required to provide and what your tenant is required to do. Know how large a security deposit you can charge, where you have to hold it, and how you handle the return of the deposit when a tenant moves out of the house.

Learn what steps you need to take if a tenant refuses to pay their rent. Hopefully, you will not use this information often. In renting to hundreds of tenants, I have had to evict only six tenants.

More of my tenants have had problems, but by quickly addressing those problems, I avoided using the court system to evict. If you have a problem with a tenant, your recourse will be in your local courts, and the process is guided by your state statutes. By understanding and complying with your state statutes, you can avoid going to court, except in cases where the tenants refuse to negotiate.

Federal fair housing (antidiscrimination) laws apply to renting and selling houses. A copy can be found online by searching for the Fair Housing Act or, again, in your public library. Read the Fair Housing Act to learn how it affects you as a residential landlord. It prohibits discrimination in the sale or rental of a house based on race, color, religion, sex, familial status, or national origin and explains your obligations if you rent to someone with a significant handicap.

THE STEPS IN RENTING A HOUSE

Here are the steps that you take to attract, select, and rent to a good tenant.

1. Get the Property Clean and in Good Repair

Always get a house in good condition before you rent it. It's a mistake to rent a dirty house or one that needs work. When you do, you will probably get a dirty tenant who will leave you with an even dirtier house that needs even more work. Tenants may promise to do work or clean, but they rarely do it.

How much does it cost to have a house professionally cleaned in your town? Typically, it is the equivalent of only a few days' rent. Who makes the decision to rent a house? If you rent to a couple, the woman typically will be the decision maker, and women prefer a clean house (because they know who will have to clean it).

Spend the money to clean the whole house: windows, screens, closets, and cabinets. Touch up or paint the house as needed. Spruce up the yard, and make sure that the house looks good from the street. A house may be beautiful inside, but if it's a dog from the street, no one is going to stop to look in the windows.

If a house rents for $1,500 a month, it costs you about $50 a day to let it sit empty. In addition, you probably are spending money on utilities and taking the time to keep the grass cut and talking to perspective tenants.

Anticipate vacancies, and move fast to clean and spruce up your property. If you can rent a house in a week instead of a month because you paid a housecleaner and a painter a little extra to work over the weekend, you are way ahead of the person who takes several weeks to paint and clean the house himself.

2. Introduce Yourself to the Neighbors

Knowing the neighbors keeps out bad tenants. When I buy a house that I intend to rent, I always introduce myself to the neighbors and give them my name and phone number. I tell them that if a tenant causes them any kind of problem, I want to hear from them and that I will do everything I can to take care of it. I want my tenants to be good neighbors, and I want good neighbors that are there to stay.

I then tell my prospective tenants that I know the neighbors and that they keep an eye on the house for me. A prospective tenant who was planning on sneaking several more roommates in or using the house for a business or an illegal purpose will not want to rent a house that is so well monitored. Such a person will leave and rent a different house.

3. Set the Rent and the Deposit

Before you begin to rent a house, write down the rent, the deposit, and the amount of income that a tenant would need to afford your house. Typically, a tenant can afford to pay between 30 and 40 percent of her income as rent. If they have other obligations, car payments, and so on, they may need more income. Some tenants will want to rent a house that they cannot afford. It is up to you to use good judgment and not allow potential tenants to obligate themselves to too much rent.

Setting the rent and deposit is not an exact science, and you can give yourself a range rather than an absolute number for a tenant's income. Charge a security deposit that is an amount greater than a month's rent. If it is the same as a month's rent, tenants will assume that they can use it to pay the last month's rent. The only money that helps you as a landlord is money you have left after the tenant moves out. The bigger the security deposit you have, the more the tenant will want it back, and the more cooperative that tenant will be.

Research your state tenant and landlord laws to see if there are restrictions on the amount of the security deposit you can charge. Most states allow a deposit of at least a month and a half's rent, and many allow two months' rent.

While you are better off with the biggest deposit you can charge, tenants will only pay so much. They will pay a larger deposit to get a better house at a fair rent. A bigger deposit will eliminate many financially marginal tenants. By charging a larger deposit, at least a month and a half's rent, you can rent to a tenant who is financially stronger and is smart enough to pay a little higher deposit to get a better house.

Monthly Rent	Tenants' Monthly Income Range	Security Deposit
$750	$1,875 to $2,500	$1,125 to $1,500
$1,000	$2,500 to $3,750	$1,500 to $2,000
$1,500	$3,750 to $5,000	$2,250 to $3,000
$2,000	$5,000 to $6,000	$3,000 to $4,000
$2,500	$6,000 to $7,500	$4,500 to $5,500

The figures shown here are just for illustration and you should adjust your criteria based on your market, and for other financial obligations that the tenants may have.

Look at both the quantity and quality of the income. Some tenants make too much money to rent your house. They can afford it easily, but they also can afford to buy, and, typically, they will buy and will only rent the house for a short time.

The quality of a tenant's income with a new job or working in a new field is lower than a tenant with a longer-term job. Commission income is a lower quality than one paid by the hour or on salary. Ask potential tenants where they work and how long they have worked there. Ask for both their income and their immediate supervisor's name and phone number. *Verify what they tell you.*

4. When the Rental Market Is Soft, Lower Your Rent, Not Your Standards

When the rental market is soft (there are many houses for rent and not many qualified tenants to rent them), rather than lowering your standards, reduce your rent to attract a quality tenant who recognizes a bargain. There are always some good tenants looking for a house. To attract them, you need a good house in a good neighborhood that is attractively priced. When you calculate the cost of letting your house sit empty for a month, it is a far better strategy to price your house on the low side of the market to begin with and to attract the best available tenant immediately rather than pricing it higher and waiting longer for a qualified tenant.

If a house rents for $1,400 a month and sits empty for a month before you rent it, it costs you $1,400 plus the cost of advertising and maintaining the house. Renting it the first week at $1,300 a month will make you more money and take less of your time. When you have an empty house, in addition to advertising and maintaining it, you have to answer the phone and interview prospective tenants. This takes a lot of your time. Otherwise, you could use the time to find another good deal.

Try to reduce the rent, not the deposit. Although the two move together, you don't want to rent to someone who cannot afford your house. The best test of this is whether the potential tenants have money in the bank today.

5. Place a Sign on the Property

You get better-qualified tenants with a sign. You get people who want to rent in that neighborhood and maybe on that street, because they have friends or family in the area. Use a good-looking sign with your phone number in larger numbers. Put an information sheet showing the price and features of the house in a front window. Leave the blinds and drapes open so that prospective tenants can see the interior. Put a message on your voice mail stating the rent and deposit and availability, and if pets are welcome.

6. Advertise on the Internet and, If Necessary, in the Newspaper

The Internet is a constantly evolving way to attract potential tenants. Different sites and technology provide ways to reach the world. The downside is that you may get fifty or more responses, and replying to fifty people with questions takes a lot of time.

I've learned to use e-mail to sort the better prospects. By asking them questions via e-mail, I avoid trying to reach them by phone and the time that that would take. Questions like "How long do you want to rent for?" "How many people will live in the house?" and "What pets do you own?" can allow you to communicate with them quicker and you'll have a written record of their responses.

Whether you advertise online or in the paper, clarify these important points: the rent, the cost to move in, the location, the size, and the condition of the property. Pictures sell. Study professional pictures of houses for sale and then mimic them.

7. Notify the Neighbors

Send the neighbors a short letter or postcard and tell them the rent amount in case they have friends looking for a place to live.

8. Arrange for Lawn Care During Vacancy

Keep the outside looking good. Try to use a neighborhood kid or local service to mow, and the worker(s) also will keep an eye on the house for you.

9. Answer Your E-mail and Phone

Some landlords use a dedicated cell phone for calls on ads. If you cannot answer it, put recorded information about the house and about how prospective tenants can contact you, either during office hours or at an open house that you have scheduled.

10. Showing the Property

Rather than meeting prospective tenants at the house, tell them to drive by the house, look in the windows if it is vacant, and then to give you a call back if they want to see the inside. If they have seen the outside and want the house, ask them to meet you to fill out an application and to leave a deposit. (I currently ask for a $100 deposit that I will refund if I don't rent to them or that I will apply to the rent if I do rent to them.)

After you have met them and they have filled out an application and you like them, then you can meet them at the house or give them a key to the house to inspect it. If you give them a key, have them sign a receipt that says, "We agree not to occupy the house, to lock the house when we leave, that no one will smoke in the property, and that we will turn off any lights, water, etc., before leaving, that we will return the key within ____ hours, and we are responsible for any damage to the house." Don't worry about theft. If someone is going to steal something out of your house, they are not going to fill out an application first; they will just break into the house.

11. Holding Open Houses

An alternative is to hold an open house at the rental house at a certain time and invite all who are interested to meet you there. Pick a time that will work for most tenants. Between 4:30 and 6:00 p.m. is a good time for most. You can do this once a week or more often depending on the number of calls you get and how eager you are to rent the house. Put a note in the window of the house with the time and date. Bring applications and rental agreements with you. Come prepared to rent the house.

12. Have the Prospective Tenant Fill Out an Application

Once prospective tenants have seen a house and want it, have them fill out a rental application. Check with your local investor's association or apartment owner's association for locally used forms and rental contracts. Another source may be a local real estate attorney who hands out free forms to drum up business. Many forms are available online. (Professional Publishing LLC has both applications and residential rental contracts at a reasonable cost.)

If your application does not ask how long the prospective tenants intend to stay, you ask them, without giving them clues to the answer that you want. The right answer is "the rest of our lives," but most tenants say one or two years. Obviously, two years is a better answer; I want people who will unpack and stay a while. The longer they stay the more money they make for me.

Ask prospective tenants for an application fee with their application. I ask for $100, which I refund if I refuse to rent them the house or apply to the security deposit if I rent to them. State laws vary on how much you can charge for application fees and security deposits. Get a copy of your state landlord-tenant statute and become knowledgeable about the sections that deal with residential leases.

13. Check Prospective Tenants' References

Call the prospective tenants' employer(s) to confirm employment and income, and call their current and immediate past landlords to ask whether they would rent to these tenants again. To make sure that you are really talking to the right person, confirm the facts that the tenants gave you. For example, the tenants may have stated that they had paid $1,000 a month rent and had lived in the previous property three years. Ask the landlord the amount of rent and how long the tenants have lived there. If it's just a friend of the tenant instead of the landlord, he may not know the answers.

14. Interview the Tenants

Before you agree to rent prospective tenants a house, you want to spend some time with them and interview them. You want them to see you as a competent landlord who has rules and wants to rent his house to tenants who will take care of the house and be good neighbors.

Part of the interview is just getting to know them. Ask where they are from, where they went to school, how many kids they have, where their family lives, what activities their kids are involved in, why they like this house and this neighborhood, and so on.

Invite the entire family to the interview so that you can see how the parents interact with the kids. Well-adjusted kids squirm and want their parents' attention. The way in which the parents handle their children shows you how the family interacts.

Always ask the kids, not the parents, what pets they have. Sometimes parents forget to list the pets on the application. The kids will tell you all about their pets.

This "small talk" will allow you to learn much more than what the prospective tenants listed on the application. You want to rent to real people who can answer these normal questions comfortably.

When you are interviewing potential tenants, ask them if they have had any credit problems. Most tenants will tell you if they do, because they assume that you are going to check.

Some new landlords are looking for the perfect tenant. Call other landlords in your town, and you will find some who want a tenant without children or pets, a nonsmoking, nondrinker, with a steady job and good credit.

Such tenants may be out there looking for a house, but they are few and far between. Most of my tenants have both kids and pets, and many have some credit problems. I like tenants with all three because they stay longer. They need me more than I need them. With a little training, they can become great tenants.

There are many honest, hardworking tenants looking for houses, but they are by no means perfect. Look for tenants who can look you in the eye and answer your direct questions. Watch for body language and how the spouse and kids react. Normal couples will both have questions. Questions are a good sign. Tenants who have no questions and are anxious to sign are desperate for a house. Keep talking to them until you find out why. If you don't like the reason, don't rent to them.

Look for signs of stability, such as staying a long time at a job or several years with a previous landlord. Ask them why they are moving. If their reason is that their current landlord won't fix anything, you might wonder why so many things needed fixing. Dig in and ask more questions about what needed fixing and why.

A tenant who needs a place tonight is not a good planner. Have them rent a motel for a day or two until you can check them out. If they cannot afford a motel, they cannot afford your house. Perhaps they have to move today because they were evicted. Stable people plan ahead more than one day for a move.

15. Collect a Cash Deposit or a Cashier's Check Made Out to You

In William Nickerson's classic book on real estate investing, *How I Turned $1,000 into a Million in Real Estate in My Spare Time*, he advised to never accept anything but cash for a security deposit. Nickerson was a hands-on landlord, and his book is still a good read for investors.

Always get your houses in good shape before you rent them, and then always require cash or a cashier's check with a current date drawn on a local bank for the deposit. (You can stop payment on a cashier's check—beware of ones with old dates.) If you make the mistake of letting tenants move in and you take a bad check for the rent and deposit, you will have to evict to get them out. That will take you a month or more. Because they did this intentionally (and fraudulently), they are unlikely to return your house to you clean and in good condition.

Tenants are creative and want you to accept something other than money for the deposit. Tenants with no money will try to talk you into renting them a house. Their pitch is that "they will take the house in its current deplorable condition [it's actually in good shape] and do all the work it needs instead of paying a deposit or first month's rent." Recognize this technique, and don't accept a story in the place of money.

16. Give the Keys, a Copy of the Rental Agreement, and an Inspection Sheet to Tenants Only After the Full Deposit and Rent Have Been Paid

Do not let tenants begin to move in until they have paid you all that they owe you.

17. Cancel Ads and Remove the Sign

If you have more than one house for rent, callers from one sign can rent the other house. You may decide to leave the sign up until the tenants move in, to generate more calls.

18. Note the Return—or Lack Thereof—of the Inspection Sheet

Always require new tenants to fill out and return to you an inspection sheet that shows the condition of the house the day they moved in. Give them only a few days to return this to you, and explain that if they fail to return it, they are stating that the house is in good condition. If there is something that needs attention, get it fixed as soon as possible.

19. Note the Deposit Amount and Rent Amount on a Bookkeeping Sheet

Circle the deposit in red so that you do not accidentally include it in your income. The security deposit is not taxable income but can be reported accidentally that way unless you are careful to note it. Learn your state laws that govern how you must handle security deposits. Some states require you to hold them in a separate account.

20. Note the Rental Amount and Due Date on Your Monthly Checklist

Have a paper checklist that lists your properties by tenants, rental amount, and due date. Have your rents all come due on the same day of the month. Most use the first because it is easier for tenants to remember. When you rent a house, prorate the first month's rent to have it fall due on the first day of the next month. If the tenants are moving in the last half of the month, collect a full month's rent and then prorate the next month's rent.

21. Have a System to Remind You When the Agreement Expires

Plan to renew and evaluate the monthly rent prior to the expiration date.

SELECTING THE RIGHT TENANTS

After reading the Fair Housing Act, make your rules for selecting tenants comply with the federal rules. As a landlord, you can still have standards. You just need to apply those standards equally to everyone.

Attracting and Training Long-Term, Low-Maintenance Tenants

What is really important to you as a landlord? If you agree with my list, the top three qualities are (1) you want someone who will pay the rent on time, (2) will take care of the property, and (3) will stay "forever." You can select your tenants based on both their history of accomplishing these actions and their potential for future performance on these important issues.

You can refuse to rent to a tenant who cannot afford your house. Before you begin the process of renting a house, set the rent and deposit amount, and tell every person who calls the same information. Not renting to someone who cannot afford your house is not discrimination; it is good business. You simply need to treat all applicants equally.

Likewise, if you require that a tenant has a certain level of income to rent your house, write down how much that will be for this house, and again, treat everyone equally. You can require proof of income, but do it for everyone.

Gross income is not the only consideration. The debt or other obligations potential tenants have, such as car or furniture payments, affect their ability to pay. The number of children and other dependents they have or other extraordinary expenses, such as a hospital debt they are obligated to repay, make them a higher-risk tenant.

Many potential tenants have some credit problems. These problems may be preventing them from buying a house. Some credit problems are a result of a catastrophe, such as a divorce, an automobile accident, or a business failure. If the prospective tenants are recovering and are able to pay their current bills, then they may be good risks as tenants. Most tenants have had some financial problems, or they would not be tenants.

You can refuse to rent to tenants who are abusing their current residence, because they likely will abuse yours. The way tenants maintain their car is also an indication of how they will maintain your house. ***Look at their car and, if possible, go inspect the house in which they live.*** You want to rent to responsible tenants who will maintain your house. You can require them to do this with your agreement, but if they are unwilling or incapable of taking care of your house, you don't want to rent to them.

Third, you are looking for tenants with long-term potential. My average tenant stays five years or more. If they stay at least two years, they have made me a profit. Tenants who move out in a year cost me money. It is expensive to have tenants move out and replace them with another. It may cost you thousands of dollars depending on how long it takes you to find a replacement tenant. Although you never really know how long someone will stay, you can look for signs of potential stability.

Ask these questions on your application: How long have you lived in your current residence? How long did you live in your previous residence? What were the addresses? (If they can't remember the addresses, they weren't there very long.)

Ask for the current and previous landlords' names and phone numbers. Often the previous landlord may be a better source of information than a current landlord, who may be happy for them to move. Call the previous landlord and ask one simple question: "Would you rent to these tenants again?" If the landlord says no, ask why.

Job stability and the type of job a prospective tenant has are additional clues to potential longevity. If they have a history of job-related transfers, they are a higher-risk tenant.

RENTING TO YOUR FIRST TENANT

The first time you rent a house, you are likely to be confused about how to screen and select tenants. When tenants call on your ad, tell them the amount of the rent and the deposit. Some will ask if they can pay over time, and others will tell you that you are charging too much. Neither of these tenants has the money to move into your house.

You are better off with an empty house than with a house occupied by tenants who cannot afford to pay the rent. Set standards and stick with them.

Ask everyone for proof of income. If a tenant is a salesperson or self-employed, require two years' tax returns. Make sure that they are signed copies of the original. Call references and confirm income if the tenant is employed.

Just before you conduct your interview, go back and review this chapter, and write down your requirements for a tenant for this house.

Most new landlords are concerned about how they can turn down tenants they don't want to rent to. Turn them down because of a business reason, not a personal reason. Here are some business reasons you can use to turn down a tenant who does not qualify to rent your house:

1. They will not fill out an application.
2. They will not give you an application fee.
3. They do not have enough money for the first month's rent and the security deposit.

4. They do not make enough money to afford the rent.
5. They do not have a verifiable source of income.
6. They do not have a steady record of employment.
7. They do not have a good history as a tenant.
8. They cannot give you a referral that you can contact.
9. They do not plan to stay as long as you want a tenant to stay.
10. They have a big dog (or several dogs or cats—or any animals you don't like—animals are not a protected class).
11. They have too many vehicles or a large truck or motor home.

This is not an all-inclusive list, but it will give you an idea of the types of reasons you can use to turn down a tenant.

In summary, you want to rent to a tenant who has a verifiable source of income that is large enough to afford your house. A tenant with long-term potential is preferable to a better-looking tenant who likely will move in six months. A tenant who moves in less than two years is costing you money. Set your goal to have your average tenant stay at least three years, and you will be a happy and successful landlord.

REWARDING YOUR GOOD TENANTS WITH FINANCIAL INCENTIVES

In my first years of renting houses, another landlord shared a technique that he used to collect rent on time. Rather than charging a late penalty like most landlords, he gave his tenants a discount for paying on or before the first of the month. The amount of the discount was meaningful enough that his tenants paid him first. If they were short that month, they paid someone else late.

The concept of giving a good tenant a real discount to pay on time works well. Today, I combine the discount for on-time payment with a discount for not calling for maintenance that month. As a tenant, you have to do both— pay on time and not call for maintenance—to earn your discount.

With this approach, tenants may just defer maintenance for months or even years. To use this discount approach safely, you also must collect a substantial security deposit and inspect your homes periodically. Your rental contract should include a clause that says any deferred maintenance that is the responsibility of the tenants will be charged against the security deposit when the tenants move out of the property.

The concept of giving a financial incentive works so well with good tenants that you rarely see them. Some of my tenants have been with me for more than twenty years—really. And during that time they have paid on time every month. These tenants are making me a lot of money and, just as important, not taking any of my time.

Other ways to reward exemplary tenants is for you to agree to pay for improvements or additions to the house that benefit the tenant. Fencing in a yard, screening a porch, adding landscaping, paying for the materials to build a deck or a fence, or simply allowing the tenant to make some modifications to the house, such as wallpaper or a different color paint, bond the tenant to your house.

My tenants have re-carpeted, painted, replaced and refinished cabinets, and installed decks and patios, all at their own expense. My longest-term tenants moved into a new house I had built twenty-six years ago and plan on living there for as long as they can.

Not every tenant will be a great tenant, but when you get one, take good care of him with reasonable rent raises and prompt responses to normal maintenance problems. Long-term tenants are worth tens of thousands of dollars to you, because they keep you from having vacancies and keep your repair bills lower. You will spend most of your money as a landlord when you have tenant turnover. Do what you can to minimize it.

BEING A SUCCESSFUL LANDLORD, WITHOUT WORKING NIGHTS OR WEEKENDS

Many people avoid buying real estate because they fear getting a phone call from a tenant in the middle of the night. I don't take a tenant's call at home. In fact, I insist that my tenants e-mail me with maintenance requests. The e-mail gives me a written record, and a chance to contact whoever will make the repair before I respond. When I call or e-mail a tenant and tell her that help is on the way, she is pleased.

Early on I decided to work no more hours than my banker does, and he does not work nights or weekends. You can be a success as a landlord and work no harder or longer than your banker.

In the rare event of an actual emergency, furnish your tenants with a list of numbers for emergency contacts. I have had five actual emergencies in managing hundreds of tenants: two fires (solution: call 911), two break-ins (solution: call the police), and a flood caused by a broken pipe (solution: call the plumber).

Not everything that a tenant would see as an emergency is an emergency to me. For example, several years ago on Thanksgiving morning one of my tenants could not get her oven to work. She thought it was an emergency, called my office number, and left a message. Since it was not a true emergency, I did not respond until the following Monday. If I had called her Thanksgiving morning, she would have been upset with me if I could not fix her oven in time for her to cook her turkey. It would have been nearly impossible—and very expensive—to find a repair person who would make a house call on Thanksgiving morning.

By the time I called her on the Monday morning after Thanksgiving, she had forgotten why she had called. The moment had passed. The "emergency" was over, and we could deal with the minor repair rationally, not emotionally.

Most "emergencies," like a hot water heater not heating, an air conditioner that is not cooling properly, or a drain line that is plugged, are not real emergencies and can be handled during business hours.

Real emergencies include fires, storm damage like a tree falling on a roof and creating a leak, a plumbing problem flooding the house, an electrical problem that is dangerous, a break-in where the house cannot be secured, and other problems that may result in injury to tenants or others.

You can delegate to tenants the responsibility for clogged drain lines (which they clogged), damaged screens or broken windows (which they damaged or broke), and anything else that they break. You can have them coordinate the repair of almost anything else—after you authorize it.

A couple of years ago I came to work on Monday morning, and a neighbor had left a message that the police had raided one of my houses and kicked in the front door. I tried calling the tenant and got no response, so I drove out to see the house. By the time I arrived, the tenant had purchased and installed a new front door to replace the one the police had damaged. It turns out that he had a problem that warranted the police arresting him, but he made bail, fixed the door, and lived there for many months until the judge sent him to jail.

Although the tenant was in trouble with the authorities, he valued his home and wanted to continue living in it. I had treated him fairly and had provided him a good place to live at a fair price. He knew that he had an obligation to fix things that he damaged, so he fixed the front door and con-tinued to pay the rent until he moved out.

BEING FIRM AND FAIR WITH TENANTS WHO TEST YOU

Tenants will test your system. If you give them a discount for paying by the first of the month, they will bring or mail the discounted amount in to you so that you receive it on the second of the month. If you accept it and still let them take the discount, the next month it will come on the fifth and then the tenth, and so on. If you give someone a financial incentive for good behavior, don't reward bad behavior. Be nice, but smile like your banker would smile if you tried to talk him out of a late charge on your monthly payment. Tell such tenants that you hope that they pay on time next month so that they can qualify for the discount. Collect the full rent on the appointed day, or you are training them to pay late.

MOVE-IN AND MOVE-OUT INSPECTIONS

Likewise, tenants will test you and ask you to do repairs that are their respon-sibility. When they do, be fair but firm. When tenants move into a house, I give them a detailed inspection sheet, which I ask them to fill out and return to me within three days of taking occupancy. I want it back quickly so that I have an accurate record of the condition of the house. I already have on file the previous tenants' sheet, and now I can compare them. The new tenants are doing the exit inspection for the old tenants, and they will be thorough.

After the three-day period, I hold the tenants accountable for any damage to the property. If they clog up the plumbing or break something, it is their responsibility to handle the maintenance call and repair on their own without involving me. If they do involve me, they will lose their discount and still may be responsible for the repair if they are at fault.

CONSISTENCY AND CONTROL— THE KEYS TO EFFECTIVE MANAGEMENT

A good property manager does not have to think a lot. He just needs to have a good set of policies and procedures and then follow them. If you find yourself making up a new answer for every tenant question, then you need to think through your policies, write them down, and be consistent with all your tenants.

Landlords get into trouble when they treat tenants differently. Establish policies and then stick with them.

The secret to being a happy, successful landlord can be summed up in a word—*control.* Many people who invest in real estate do it because they like to be in control of their investments. Landlords who are miserable have lost control. Their tenants are running the show.

TRAINING YOUR TENANTS

Either you will train your tenants, or they will train you. I use the word *train* here not as in training a pet simply to respond to a command. Rather, tenants will learn what they can expect from you, when you respond to their requests, or when they test your system of management.

Good tenants are looking for fair and responsive landlords. Being fair and responsive will not necessarily cost you money. In fact, if prospective tenants believe that you are both fair and responsive, they are more likely to rent from you. Many landlords are neither.

To be in control as a landlord, you need a management system that both you and your tenants understand and that you implement. Like teenagers, tenants will search for boundaries and then test them. As the landlord, you need to set those boundaries clearly. When you are tested, restate the boundaries and be fair but firm in sticking with the rules.

Training starts with your first contact with prospective tenants and continues through your entire relationship with them. You set the stage with your rental application and initial interview. After that, your response to requests will train people to either call more often or to handle their own problems.

It is important that you have policies, that your policies comply with the law, and that you enforce those policies. In more than thirty years of managing hundreds of tenants and studying other successful landlords, I have established the following rules as policy for renting houses. Use them and they will save you thousands of dollars and many hours of aggravation.

Single-Family House Management Policies

1. Always get cash (or a local cashier's check or money order) for the first month's rent and the security deposit. (Never accept an old or out-of-town cashier's check—they may have stopped payment on it.)

2. Never accept a partial security deposit and allow a tenant to have possession of the house. Prorate the rent, and take a full deposit. (You cannot evict for nonpayment of deposit.)

3. Always use an all-inclusive rental agreement with which you are comfortable and understand fully. Never negotiate the agreement with tenants. If they win this negotiation, they will negotiate more.

4. Always take the time to go over the entire agreement with all adults who will be living in the house. Try to interview the entire family.

5. Never discriminate. Treat every tenant and applicant equally and fairly. Do not bend policies because a tenant belongs to a minority. Treat *everyone* the same.

6. Have a late payment policy and stick with it. When you make an exception, the exception will soon become the rule.

7. Always serve late tenants with notices as soon as they are late.

8. Feeling sorry for tenants doesn't help them or you. Pay them to move out; take action! Do not confuse business with charity, or you may not have the money to be charitable.

9. Keep good records of all income and receipts. Always give receipts for rent collected in cash; keep duplicate copies in a receipt book.

10. Respond to tenant requests in a reasonable and businesslike manner. Distinguish between ordinary maintenance and real emergencies. Have a system in place to handle true emergencies.

11. Keep the property in good repair, and inspect the outside of a property several times a year to ensure that tenants are taking care of the property.*

GETTING RID OF PROBLEM TENANTS

The primary reason to move tenants out of a property before the term is up is that they are not paying rent. Take immediate action when tenants do not pay on time. Deliver to them a three-day pay or quit (i.e., move) notice. It is the first step in the eviction process. Read your state's statutes so that you know in advance what actions you need to take.

---

*Reprinted from John Schaub's "Building Wealth One House at a Time—Beyond the Book Seminar," 2016, by permission of Pro Serve Corporation of Sarasota, Inc.

When tenants receive this prompt response to their nonpayment, typically they will pay you. If they don't pay you, the next step is to talk with them, if possible, to see if you can work out a payment schedule that they can afford.

Sometimes, converting tenants to a weekly pay schedule (at a higher rent) will make it possible for them to stay in the house. Take the monthly rent and divide it by four, and have the tenants begin to pay you this new amount *every Friday*. Since there are fifty-two Fridays in a year (not $4 \times 12 = 48$), you will receive an extra four weeks' rent each year for your trouble.

If this solution does not solve the problem, offer to return a portion of the security deposit if they move immediately. You can make the offer this way: "I can hire an attorney to evict you, in which case you will lose your entire deposit, or I can give you part of your deposit back if you will move out by next Friday. Would you rather I pay you or an attorney?"

You must make this offer short-term so that if they do not move as agreed, you still have enough deposit to protect you if you have to continue on with the eviction process. It's worth repeating myself and saying that I have had only six evictions in managing hundreds of tenants. The secret of having few evictions is a good selection process coupled with an immediate response when a tenant does not pay. An eviction is the most expensive way to move a tenant out.

RAISING YOUR RENTS

You Cannot Raise Your Rent on an Empty House

The first step in raising the rent is having a full house. If you own a dozen full houses, you can constantly test the market by raising one rent each month. If tenants start moving out because they can find a cheaper, comparable house, then stop raising them for a while.

Raising your rents a little bit every year is good for you and your tenants. Your costs will go up most years. Your tenants expect some increase—the secret of keeping your tenants long-term is a series of small increases.

Consider how a good tenant paying you $1,200 a month would react if you did not raise his rent for five years and then one year you jumped it $300 a month. The $300 a month increase may not even catch him up to market rent, but it still will be a shock to him, and he may move. This would cost you a good tenant and the tenant a good home.

It would be better for you and the tenant to raise his rent $75 every year. Over five years you would actually raise rents more, but your good tenants won't move to avoid a $75 yearly increase in rent. It costs far more than that to move, not to mention the aggravation of moving.

Track your tenants, and raise their rents a fair amount once a year. If there is a season of the year that tenants hate to move, time your rent increases to fall in that season, and fewer will move.

If the rental market is soft and you want to keep your good tenants, put a handwritten note on the rent increase letter to call you if they have any questions. If they call and say that they will have to move if you raise the rent, you may decide to leave the rent alone this year to keep a good tenant.

During recessions, I have lowered my rents to keep my good tenants. I'd rather be 100 percent full at 90 percent of market rent than 10 percent empty trying to get 100 percent of market rent.

When your houses are full of solid tenants, you can spend your time looking for good deals rather than trying to rent houses. A landlord who tries to squeeze the top dollar in rent out of a lot of his houses will spend a lot of time looking for new tenants.

Set your rents slightly below the market, charge a larger-than-average security deposit, keep your houses in good shape, and you can attract the best tenants in your town.

AVOIDING LANDLORD BURNOUT

Some landlords enjoy owning property all their life. In fact, owning and managing property is something you can do as long as you want to. Many of my more senior students are well into their eighties and still enjoy managing their money and their property. In doing the research for a book I coauthored entitled, *Optimal Aging* (available at www.optimalaging.com), I found that staying active in managing your financial affairs keeps you young and that you will often make better decisions than those to whom you delegate.

Other landlords suffer "burnout" and sell their property before they benefit from long-term appreciation and debt payoff.

There are a couple of keys to avoiding landlord burnout. The first is buying property that attracts long-term tenants who have the same value system that you do. You want to rent to tenants who see themselves as homeowners one day. These tenants will value the house they live in, and they may want a reference from you to either buy a house or to rent another.

There are big differences in how people view themselves and others. If you rent to people who are constantly trying to beat you out of the rent, eventually you will wear out.

Another key is avoiding high-turnover, high-management property. Renting low-income property to tenants who can't afford anything better is a hard way to make a fortune. People who live on the edge of financial disaster are high-management tenants. They often cannot pay the rent for if they miss even one day's pay.

The third key is to buy the right number of properties for you. Set your goals in terms of cash flow and net worth, not in terms of numbers of properties. You may decide that you only need a few properties. Fewer properties mean fewer tenants and less work.

18

KNOWING WHEN TO SELL AND HOW TO SELL

The longer you hold a house that is appreciating and producing cash flow, the more money it will make you. However, there are reasons and a time to sell your investments.

BEFORE YOU SELL, ANSWER THESE QUESTIONS

1. What is your market doing today? Are properties selling quickly? Is the inventory down and are prices moving up? If so it's an opportunity to sell your weaker properties.

    If prices are declining, ask why. Is it because of a significant event that will affect your housing market long term, like a large business or military base closing causing a drop in population? Or is the downturn due to overbuilding, or a change in the credit market?

    If you think it will be many years before prices come back, selling today and buying back in at cheaper prices may be a good decision. But kicking out good tenants, and giving up the income, is giving up a lot. Before you sell, know your after-tax net. If your houses are in good shape and have long-term tenants, holding through a recession is often a better strategy than trying to sell at the top and buy back at the bottom.

2. What is happening on the streets where you own property? Properties on different streets within a neighborhood, are constantly changing. Study each street where you own and determine whether holding for five more years is a good plan. Neighborhoods improve and property values increase when landlords or banks sell to owners who then fix up houses. Neighborhoods decline and property values drop when landlords or banks let properties deteriorate.

3. Does your house have a long-term tenant in residence or a record of attracting long-term tenants? If so, it is cranking out cash flow for you.

   In the long run, your profits from cash flow will often be greater than your profits from appreciation. Rents go up with inflation, just like prices. As my house prices have climbed from $50,000 to $200,000, my rents have increased from $400 to $1,600 on those same houses. The big difference is that I get the rent every month but have to wait until I sell for the appreciation. Said another way, *the profits from the rents that I receive today are much more valuable to me than the profit I will receive ten years from now*.

4. Can you refinance today on good terms? I like owning property free and clear but am also a big fan of monthly cash flow. If I can refinance a loan and increase my cash flow, I do. If you increase your cash flow when you refinance, you reduce your risk from having debt. Debt is risky when you cannot repay it.

   Refinancing is a great strategy when you can pay off one or more loans with high payments with one new low-payment loan. I refinanced one house with a new low-interest-rate, thirty-year loan and paid off three older loans with high payments. My one, new loan payment was less per month than my previous payment. Plus, I ended up with two free-and-clear houses.

5. Is your house in rentable shape and does it operate with reasonable maintenance costs? Most foreclosures and short sales I look at are not in good enough shape to attract a decent tenant. Some landlords are renting houses without getting them into good condition, but I've found that when you advertise a nasty-looking house for rent, the tenants you attract look a lot like the house.

6. Is your rental market strong? When we have tenants competing for houses, it is a good time to rent, not sell, your houses. Rents go up in spurts. Remember, you will often make more from the rents than appreciation.

7. Is the house located close to where you live or work? At one time I owned property in ten states, and that was an education. I learned that I made more money and spent less time traveling when my properties were in my town. Over the years, I have disposed of everything out of state and now will not buy a house unless it's within a ten-minute drive of my office.

   Unless you live where no one makes money investing in real estate, learn to invest where you live, or move to where it is easier. My favorite Jim Rohn quote is, "Don't wish it was easier, wish you were better."

   It is not as easy if you live in a higher-priced market, but if you get better, you will make a lot more money than an investor who lives in a low-priced market. Many of my most successful students started with little money in very expensive markets, such as Orange County, California. Today they own houses worth many times what my houses are worth, and, predictably, their cash flow is higher than mine. It takes far fewer houses to make you rich in an expensive market.

8. Are there some houses that you own today that you want to keep forever? If not, do you want to acquire one or more properties that you will own for the rest of your life?

What qualifies a house as one that you want to "keep forever"?

Houses that attract long-term, low-maintenance tenants.

Houses that are well built and have lower-than-average maintenance costs.

Houses with taxes and insurance that are in line with the rents.

Houses with a low-interest, long-term loan or are free and clear, that will produce cash flow even at reduced rents.

Houses that are located in neighborhoods that are improving.

GOOD REASONS TO SELL A HOUSE

Houses grow old, neighborhoods change, and landlords get tired. Here are some good reasons to sell a house:

1. *Neighborhood changing for the worse.* Neighborhoods have cycles. When owners sell out and landlords buy many houses in a neighborhood, property values often will drop. Sell when you see this happening.

2. *Worn-out house.* It costs a lot of money and takes a lot of time to fix up a house that needs a new kitchen, baths, plumbing, roof, and so on. Most improvements you make only increase the value of a house by a fraction of what you spend. An investment in a new kitchen, one of the best things you can do, will increase the value of the house only by about 75 percent of what you spend. It is smarter to buy another house in good repair and sell your worn-out house to a buyer looking for a project. There are a lot of buyers in that category.

3. *Worn-out landlord.* Some landlords enjoy their work into their eighties. It is one job that you can keep for life if you want it. A skilled landlord with twenty properties may work only an hour or two a month. You can delegate all the bad jobs and keep the ones that you like. Should you reach the point where you are not having any fun, consider selling to a family member whom you can teach the business or to another, younger investor. See more details below.

4. *The house is far away.* I obviously prefer to invest in my own back yard. If you own a property in a faraway town, you have to weigh the benefits or cost of holding it until the market improves against selling it now. If you have a loss, you may consider selling it for a loss that could offset the profit you could make from selling another property for a gain.

5. *The house loses money.* Whenever I find myself with a losing property, I am aggressive about selling it. I'd rather take a loss today and be free to pursue another opportunity than try to squeeze a few more dollars out of a losing investment. It may be a loser because of bad financing, or bad construction, or bad neighbors. Unless I can fix it quickly and at a cost that makes sense, I sell and buy another, better property.

SELLING FOR THE WRONG REASONS

It can be a mistake to sell. Once you have bought a property that makes you money every month, don't sell it unless it is part of your plan.

1. *You have an empty house.* If it has attracted good tenants in the past, don't sell, hold it. If it does not attract well-behaved, long-term tenants,

then selling an empty house is better than selling one with a tenant in it. Tenants are not an asset when you sell, because it is not in their best interest. They may have to move. Because of this, they may not cooperate in showing the house, and it may not look its best. Most buyers will not want to move in.

2. *No leverage.* I have had financial advisors tell me that owning free-and-clear properties is a terrible idea, and they are right, to a point. They say the rate of return is low. What they do not consider is that if you own ten houses, you can own five of them free and clear and five with loans, and increase your rate of return with the leverage.

   Once you have enough property to produce all the cash flow you need, your focus should be to pay off your debt, not borrow more. It is easier to borrow money than to pay it back. If your strategy is to refinance, do it when rates are low.

3. *No depreciation.** If you own a house long enough, you will run out of depreciation. If the house is in a great neighborhood and making you money, keep it. Would you sell a stock that goes up every year and pays a big dividend? No, you wouldn't, and stocks have no depreciation. If you want more depreciation, buy more property; don't sell off your winners.

4. *Someone wants to buy your house.* Someone always will want to buy your best properties. If you are going to sell one, sell your weakest property. When you begin to acquire properties, keep a list with your favorite property at the top and your least favorite at the bottom. If you are married, share this with your spouse, and tell your spouse that if he or she ever needs to sell, sell the ones on the bottom of the list first.

HOW TO SELL

You can use an agent to sell your property or you can sell it yourself. If you have no experience selling, the agent may do a better job. If you learn how to sell property yourself, then you may be able to get as high a price as the agent and save the commission.

---

*Depreciation is an income tax deduction that allows a taxpayer to recover the cost or other basis of a house held for investment. It is an annual deduction a landlord can use to offset rental income on his or her tax return. See IRS form 4562 with the instructions for a complete explanation.

My favorite way to sell is using lease/options, as described in Chapter 15. Selling on lease/options allows me to sell to a homeowner who is struggling to buy a house, often their first house, and yet sell at a retail price. I sell the house in "as is" condition and have the buyer pay the closing cost. This increases my net profit by at least 10 percent.

A student of mine who had accumulated many houses, systematically sold his houses one at a time to young investors. He gave these investors a chance to make a profit off their first house while selling at a good price without any advertising or expense. If they did not exercise their option and close, he still owned the house. He could then renegotiate at a higher price and rent or sell to another.

SELL TO AN OWNER OCCUPANT WITH SELLER FINANCING

Owner financing, where your buyer pays you a down payment and then pays you monthly payments until he pays for the house, is similar to selling with a lease/option with a few important differences. When you sell a house using owner financing, regardless of the paperwork that you use, you have a sale for tax purposes.

That sale can be treated as an installment sale, if you qualify. An installment sale allows you to report your profit as you receive it, not all in the first year of the sale.

It is important to note that "dealer property" cannot be sold using an installment sale. Dealer property is inventory. For a builder, it's a house he is building to sell. For a "flipper," it is a house he has fixed up and is selling. If you are a builder or flipper, any sale of your inventory does not qualify. This is an important point.

You must elect to take an installment sale and file IRS Form 6252. Check with your accountant for details. See IRS Publication 537 for a complete explanation.

An advantage to the buyer is lower closing costs and a lower down payment than a bank would require. The seller needs to be able to judge whether the buyer has the income to make the payments. The Dodd-Frank Wall Street Reform and Consumer Protection Act of 2010 H.R. 4173 has regulations that apply to those who sell more than one house a year to a homeowner with owner financing. It does not apply to sales to investors. You can sell several houses with owner financing in one year to investors. You can sell multiple houses a year to owner occupants, but you must comply with the provisions of this law.

Should the buyer stop making payments, be aware of the cost to get the buyer out of the house and out of title. This may require a foreclosure. Foreclosing, like evicting, should be used only as a last resort. It is nearly always cheaper and faster to negotiate with a buyer who can no longer make his payments and to buy out his interest rather than pay an attorney to have him evicted or foreclosed. If you do this, have an attorney or title company prepare the documents.

SELLING AND REINVESTING WITHOUT PAYING A TAX ON YOUR GAIN

If you are going to sell and then invest in other investment real estate, you can defer paying any tax until you sell by making an IRC Section 1031 tax-deferred exchange. Note that the new property must be held for investment. It does not have to be the same type of investment property. You could sell a house and buy a duplex or commercial property or even land that you planned to hold as an investment. The replacement property cannot be your personal residence or a vacation home.

If you do an exchange with a related party, certain rules apply. Related parties include, but are not limited to, immediate family members, such as brothers, sisters, spouses, ancestors, and lineal descendants. Related parties do not include stepparents, uncles, aunts, in-laws, cousins, nephews, nieces, and ex-spouses.

Corporations, limited-liability companies, or partnerships in which more than 50 percent of the stock, membership interests, or partnership interests, or more than 50 percent of the capital interests or profit interests is owned by the taxpayer is also considered to be a related party.

Related parties who concurrently exchange properties with each other must hold the properties for two years following the 1031 exchange. Both related parties will recognize their respective depreciation recapture and capital gain income tax liabilities if either party disposes of its respective property within two years after the simultaneous 1031 exchange or transfer.

If you plan to use IRC Section 1031 to defer your tax, have the next property that you want to buy identified before you sell. Section 1031 currently requires you to identify your replacement property within forty-five days from your first closing and then close on it in 180 days. No extensions are allowed. The first forty-five days goes by quickly, so knowing what you want to buy and even having it under contract will improve your chances of completing the exchange.

Get good legal and tax counsel before you sign a contract to ensure that your paperwork and strategy comply with the IRS requirements.

If you sell you will owe recapture tax on the depreciation you have taken, which is 25 percent of the amount of depreciation you claimed. This is called depreciation recapture. Check with your CPA. You can avoid the recapture tax by successfully completing a Section 1031 exchange.

If you have properties with large gains, most of your profit is due to appreciation, so the amount of depreciation you have to recapture will be less significant. If you buy a house for $100,000 and hold it until you sell it for $300,000, you will only have depreciation to recapture on the part of the $100,000 that you have depreciated.

In addition to not paying taxes, an exchange forces you to reinvest your profits into another property. Keeping your investment capital invested continuously makes a huge difference in your net worth in the long run.

ACCEPT A SMALLER HOUSE AS A DOWN PAYMENT

If the house you are trying to sell is a "move up" home, then it is likely that the buyers will already be owners of a smaller house. An excellent way to make a deal is to accept their existing house as a down payment on the house you are trying to sell.

If the buyers like your house, they need to sell their house before they can buy yours. Car dealers discovered the solution to the same problem years ago. You don't have to sell your old car before you buy a new one, it is easy; they will take your old car on a trade. Do they make money on your old car? Sure.

You can make money taking a house on a trade. Remember, the seller is thinking that they will have to pay a commission and perhaps reduce their price to get their house sold. If you simply accept it as a down payment, they can avoid the trauma of having people walk through their house making disparaging remarks before receiving a low-ball offer.

If you sell your more expensive house at a retail price and accept the buyers' house as a down payment, you will make a profit.

Your house for sale price:	$225,000
Your cost in the house is:	$180,000
Buyers' house at market value:	$140,000 − 7% = $130,200
Buyers' loan balance:	$100,000

You accept their $30,200 equity as a down payment on your $225,000 house.

They get a new loan for $194,800 ($225,000 less their $30,200 equity).

You get their house subject to their loan and $194,800 in cash at the closing.

If you have a loan on your house, you will pay it with part of the cash you receive.

If they have a loan on their property, you can assume it or take title subject to the loan.

If the house is not one that you want to keep, consider selling it on a one-year lease/option. A good strategy is to take title subject to, because you will have a plan to pay off their loan in a short time (one year or less).

If you are contacted by the seller's lender, you can explain that the house is under contract and the new buyers are working on securing financing. It is exactly what a lease/option buyer should be doing. They may have a year to close, but they should not wait to qualify for a loan. Set up a meeting with a lender before you agree to sell to them to see what they need to do to qualify for a loan. Unless they have a good chance of getting a new loan, don't sell to them on a lease/option.

KNOW HOW MUCH YOU WILL OWE IN TAXES BEFORE YOU SELL

Learn about the taxes you will owe as a result of owning and selling real estate before the sale is complete. For more practical information on how to avoid or minimize taxes, read John T. Reed's excellent book *Aggressive Tax Avoidance for Real Estate Investors* (www.johntreed.com). It is a clear explanation of tax-deferred exchanges and installment sales and is a must-read for real estate investors.

19

GETTING YOUR HOUSES FREE AND CLEAR

SETTING YOUR GOAL FOR FREE-AND-CLEAR HOUSES

The first step is to set a goal for the number of free-and-clear houses that you want to own. Work backward into this goal by first setting an income goal and then asking how many free-and-clear houses you will need to produce that target income.

For example, suppose that the house you would like to buy in your town produces rent in the $1,200 to $1,400 per month range and has operating expenses equal to about 40 percent of the gross rent. How many houses would you need?

One house (rental income $1,200 per month): $14,400 per year
Operating expenses (40 percent): $5,760 per year
Net income: $8,640 per year

Annual Income Needed	Number of Free-and-Clear Houses Needed
$50,000	6
$100,000	12
$150,000	18
$200,000	24

Use real numbers in your town, and then make a projection using today's values and income to determine how many houses you will need to earn your desired income. As rents increase with inflation, this income will provide you with the same lifestyle, even as consumer prices increase over time.

THREE PLANS FOR GETTING YOUR HOUSES FREE AND CLEAR

Plan 1: Use the Increased Cash Flow from Increasing Rents to Pay Off the Debt

How many years will it take you to pay off a thirty-year loan? Thirty years if you make the same payment each month for thirty years. If you increase the amount of the payment you make as you raise your rents; you can pay off your loans much sooner.

As you acquire property with fixed payments—amortizing loans—your cash flow will increase each year as you increase your rents. You can use the increasing cash flow from one house to pay off the debt on that house.

If your rents increase at an average of 5 percent a year and you use that increase to make additional principal payments on your loan, you can pay off a thirty-year loan in just over fourteen years. Table 19.1 shows what your payment schedule would look like if you applied your increasing rent to your loan each year. The original loan is a thirty-year $150,000 loan with 7 percent interest and payments of $997.75.

Although this is a simple plan and it works, *it is not the quickest way to pay off the debt on your houses*. A better plan is to use the cash flow that the house produces to continue to buy other houses until you have the number of houses that, if paid for, will produce the cash flow that you need.

When you pay off a loan with an interest rate of 7 percent, you are investing your money at that 7 percent rate. If you buy another house with a small down payment, the return you will make on your investment during the first few years could be 20 to 40 percent, or higher. You can then use those profits to pay off your loans, and you can pay them off faster.

Table 19.1 Paying Off Your Thirty-Year Loans
in Less Than Fifteen Years

Year	Rent Collected/Payment Made	Loan Balance at Year End
1	$997.75	$148,607
2	$1,050	$146,394
3	$1,155	$142,775
4	$1,215	$138,103
5	$1,276	$132,338
6	$1,338	$125,390
7	$1,405	$117,114
8	$1,475	$107,376
9	$1,550	$96,010
10	$1,628	$82,858
11	$1,709	$67,776
12	$1,794	$50,512
13	$1,884	$30,911
14	$1,978	$8,478
15	$2,077	$0

If you make prepayments of principal on any loan, keep careful records of your extra payments. It would be wiser and easier to keep track of if you just made one larger prepayment of principal each year rather than making increased monthly payments. For example, in year two, rather than making twelve payments of $1,050, you could make one prepayment of $600 at the end of the year. You would pay a few dollars more interest during the year, but the fourteen-year payoff plan would still work.

Bank bookkeepers do make mistakes, and when you make many unusual payments, they may not record them accurately and give you the proper credit. Keep your own records, keep proof of your payments, and make your own amortization schedule by using programs that are widely available.

Plan 2: Buy More Houses Than You Really Want and Sell Off Some to Pay Off the Rest

Knowing that you can make more than a 7 percent return when you buy a house as an investment, a better plan is to use the profits that your houses will generate to buy additional houses. This will take more work—buying and managing more houses requires more of your time and effort—but the results can be spectacular.

If, using the same cash flow as in the preceding example, you took the excess cash and bought more houses, here is an example of how the plan would work: Year 1, buy the first house. Years 2 through 10, buy another house each year using the cash flow from the earlier houses to provide down payments and to fund any cash-flow shortages in the new houses that you buy.

Remember the 10/10/10 rule? Here is an example of how the equity would grow in the first house that you bought if you did a little better than 10/10/10. You will do better as you practice making offers and learn your market.

Market value when you bought:	$180,000
Your purchase price:	$160,000
Your down payment:	$10,000
Your loan:	$150,000

Using a conservative rate of growth of 5 percent, let's look at the value and the debt after just ten years:

Projected market value (at 5 percent growth):	$320,000
Loan balance in ten years:	$125,920
Equity in property:	$194,080

It's hard to project what income tax rates will be in ten years, but even after taxes, you should be able to sell one house, gross $194,000, pay taxes, and pay off another house that will have a loan balance of about the same, $125,920.

Rather than waiting fourteen years to pay off a loan using the increased rents, this plan allows you to get a house free and clear in ten years at a conservative 5 percent rate of growth.

Plan 3: Refinance Some Property to Pay Off Others

If you follow plan 2 and continue to buy houses at below-market prices and with good financing, you will one day own a number of houses. Each will have a different loan balance and a different payment schedule. Some of these loans will have better interest rates and terms than others.

Take the time to carefully study the payments and amounts on all your loans and compare them. Which loans have the largest payments compared with the amount that you owe?

Suppose that you owned three houses with the following loans:

House	Market Value	Loan Amount	Loan Payment
1	$200,000	$100,000	$700
2	$200,000	$100,000	$900
3	$200,000	$100,000	$1,200

Without knowing the interest rate on the loans, which would you want to pay off first? Obviously, the one with the highest payments. You can invest the same $100,000 and increase your monthly cash flow by paying off the loan with the largest payment. The interest rate is not as important as the ratio between the amount that you owe and the amount of the monthly payment.

As loans get older, their balances pay down, but the monthly payments remain the same. House 3 may have started with a $150,000 loan that has been paid down to $100,000.

If you are going to refinance one or more properties to pay off another, either refinance or pay off the loans with the highest payments to increase your cash flow.

Looking again at the house in the preceding example:

Projected market value in ten years (at 5 percent growth):	$320,000
Loan balance in ten years:	$125,920
Equity in property:	$194,080

Banks generally will lend investors 80 percent of the market value when you refinance a property. If you refinanced this house with a new 80 percent loan, you would be able to borrow $256,000.

If you owned another house with about the same loan balance of $126,000, you could pay off the loans on those two houses by refinancing just one house.

Now you would own one house free and clear and one with an 80 percent loan. If you can refinance when rates are low, you should be able to cover your payment with the rent that one house produces.

Owning a house free and clear and one with an 80 percent loan is a much safer position than having a $125,000 loan against both houses. When you have a large loan balance, the lender will not want to foreclose and will work with you in the event you have financial difficulties. When you have a small loan balance, the lender will gladly foreclose, confident that they will be repaid.

Another advantage is that replacing two old loans with a new thirty-year loan will reduce your payment. If you can borrow at a lower interest rate, your payment will drop even more.

A third advantage is, because you have not sold a house, you will pay no taxes. Because you have not sold, you still have both houses earning money for you.

You can use all three strategies, depending on the market, your desire to own a certain number of properties, and your need for cash flow. One thing is certain: You will change your plan if you start today and invest for the next ten years. You will continue to learn more and will find ways to make even higher returns with your cash.

INCREASING YOUR PROFIT DRAMATICALLY WITH A PHONE CALL

Always ask for a discount when paying off any loan. This may seem strange to you, but lenders, especially private lenders and some smaller banks, want their money back sooner. To get it sooner, they will take less than the full face value—but only if you ask them to do so.

You must make this offer before they know that they will be paid off. You can ask them this way, "I was planning to pay off some of my loans, and yours was one I was considering. Would you be interested in being paid off today rather than over the next ten (use the real remaining loan balance) years? If so, my closing costs to refinance and pay you off would be $4,320. Would you be willing to pay that amount if I paid your loan off now?"

You receive discounts by asking for them. I owed one seller $10,000 due in less than one year. She offered to take a $4,000 discount to get her money nine months early. It would have been smarter for her to wait the nine months. Where else could she earn $4,000 on a $6,000 investment in nine months? I knew that I was going to pay her, but lenders never know that they are going to get paid until the check is cashed. The certainty of money today, rather than waiting for it, is worth a lot.

Check with your tax advisor on how to report any discount you are able to negotiate. The amount of the discount probably will be taxable, but if you save $4,000 and owe a tax of $1,000, you are still $3,000 ahead.

BEING EFFICIENT WHEN REFINANCING

Interest rates and the credit market have cycles. When the rates are low and credit is loose, borrowing money to restructure your existing debt or to finance new purchases can be profitable. When interest rates are high, you don't want to replace a low-interest loan with a high-interest loan.

If you are a long-term investor, you can play the cycles. When rates are low, borrow when you can refinance your debt and reduce your payments. It costs less to refinance one house than three houses. If you can, refinance just one with the most equity to get the cash you need to pay off other debt or for other investment.

INCREASING YOUR INCOME TODAY BY SPENDING SOME OF YOUR PRINCIPAL

You can increase your income even more by systematically selling some houses.

By talking to my estate attorney friends I learned that most people who accumulate significant assets during their lifetimes become more conservative as they age and end up with most of these assets in their estates.

Unless you have a reason to leave a large estate, you can sell some of your assets and spend or give away the money while you are alive. One of my favorite preachers likes to say, "Do your giving while you're living, so you're know'n where it's going." People who discover the joy of giving really get a kick out of making gifts that help others change their lives. Give while you are alive to see how your gift makes a difference.

If you supplement your rental income with income from sales of properties, you can meet your financial goals quicker and do it with fewer properties than if you depend only on the rental income.

Suppose that at age sixty you own twenty houses; ten that are free and clear and ten with amortizing loans. The loans on the ten financed houses all will be paid off within the next twenty years.

Your plan is to produce the greatest possible income during the next twenty years so that you can enjoy those years to their fullest, and then at age eighty, you want to own ten free-and-clear properties to support you comfortably for the rest of your life.

During the next twenty years, you plan to sell ten houses to increase your income, keeping the remaining ten houses for your more passive retirement years. Today, each house is worth about $150,000. Your plan is to sell one every two years on average to increase your income by about $75,000 (in today's money) per year. You can adjust this strategy to get the best prices by selling only in strong real estate markets.

Selling will reduce your workload, since you will have fewer tenants and houses to watch over. It will also reduce your rental income over time. This may be offset by increasing rents.

20

MAKING IT BIG ON LITTLE DEALS

I n my classes I have taught thousands how to buy houses for investment. Many students have made it in a very big way. Some own hundreds of houses. Others have bought a few houses to supplement or replace the income from their jobs.

To make money as an investor, you have to take risks. If the risk is small— if it is a little deal—you are more likely to take it. A modestly priced house in a good neighborhood can be an almost risk-free investment if you learn how to buy, finance, and manage it well. You can buy it with a relatively small down payment and rent it to a tenant who will pay you enough to repay your loan.

It takes a modest amount of work to find, buy, and rent a house, but the reward is more than worth the work and risk. Those who fail to take this chance, who will not make the effort to buy even a safe investment, run a far greater risk—the risk of never building any wealth. The great majority of people, even in our free and wealthy country, do not build any significant wealth. They must rely on the government, a company pension, or relatives for support.

Reduce your risk by learning before you write a check to buy your first investment. Hopefully, this book has answered some of your questions and given you the direction that you need to write that first check and buy that first house.

WRITING DOWN YOUR PLAN FOR BUILDING WEALTH

Commit today to buying at least one house in the coming year. Don't worry about what the market is doing, look for a house that you can buy using my 10/10/10 rule, and you will own a house that should rent for at least the amount of your payments. You will learn a lot and build some self-confidence in the process.

Now hold on to that house until it doubles in value. If you don't refinance it along the way, your cash flow from that house will increase every year.

All you need to do to become wealthy is to repeat the process; to buy one house a year for ten years and to hold them until they double in value (see Table 20.1).

If houses in your town double in value every ten years, Table 20.2 shows what your houses will look like in ten years if the first house you bought was worth $150,000. (If they don't double in ten years, hold them until they do.) Your first house will double in value from $150,000 to $300,000, and since you will continue to buy the same type of house in the same neighborhood, all your houses will be worth about $300,000 in ten years, or however long they take to double.

There is nothing complicated about this plan. It simply requires you to stick with it and buy one house a year and then hold on to those houses until they double in value. These numbers are conservative. As you improve your buying and borrowing skills, you will make deals better than 10/10/10.

SECRETS OF SUCCESS

Warren Buffett has made billions of dollars as an investor during my lifetime. He and I agree on most everything, and here I have restated and embellished some of his thoughts for real estate investors.

1. *Buy value.* Buy investments that have real value, and buy them at a bargain price. Buy a house you know the value of and that will produce income, and buy it when you can make a good deal.

Table 20.1 My Net Worth in Ten Years If I Buy Just One House

1. Market value of the first house you buy today: $_____
2. Using 10/10/10 buy at least 10 percent below the market: $_____
   - Put no more than 10 percent down: $_____
   - Your original loan balance: $_____
   - Your beginning equity in the house: $_____
3. Hold your first house until it doubles in value: Line 1 + 2 = $_____
4. The loan balance after 10 years on a 30-year loan is about 86 percent of the original balance: $_____
5. Your equity (value − loan balance): $_____

Here is an example using a house worth $150,000 today:

1. Market value of the first house you buy today: $150,000
2. Using 10/10/10, buy at least 10 percent below the market: $135,000
   - Put no more than 10 percent down: $13,500
   - Your original loan balance: $121,500
   - Your beginning equity in the house: $28,500
3. Hold your first house until it doubles in value: Line 1 + 2 = $300,000
4. The loan balance after 10 years on a 30-year 7 percent loan is about 86 percent of the original balance: $104,000
5. Your equity (value − loan balance): $196,000

2. *Hold on to your good investments—forever.* Don't sell a house that rents well and appreciates. It is making you a lot of money.
3. *Sell losers as soon as possible.* When you make a mistake admit it, recognize why it happened, get rid of it, and learn from the experience.
4. *Treat others as you would like to be treated.* You can make a lot of money buying, renting, and selling houses without ever making anyone angry. When you treat people well, they will send their friends your way.
5. *There is unlimited opportunity to build wealth.* Buying houses, one at a time, and holding them until they at least double in value can build you more wealth than 98 percent of your friends and neighbors, and it can do it faster than you'd believe.

Table 20.1   My Net Worth If I Buy One House a Year for Ten Years

Year	House Price in 10 Years	Approximate Loan Balance in 10 Years	Your Equity in 10 Years
1	$300,000	$104,000	$196,000
2	$300,000	$121,000	$179,000
3	$300,000	$138,000	$162,000
4	$300,000	$155,000	$145,000
5	$300,000	$172,000	$128,000
6	$300,000	$189,000	$111,000
7	$300,000	$206,000	$94,000
8	$300,000	$223,000	$77,000
9	$300,000	$235,000	$65,000
10	$300,000	$245,000	$55,000
Totals	$3,000,000	$1,788,000	$1,212,000

Get outside your comfort zone. Take a small risk on a little deal—and you can *MAKE IT BIG*!

21

THE FULLER CENTER FOR HOUSING
Helping Others Build Wealth, One House at a Time

"What the poor need is capital, not charity, co-workers, not caseworkers."

—*Millard Fuller, Co-Founder*
THE FULLER CENTER FOR HOUSING
and Habitat for Humanity

I met Millard Fuller when he spoke to a group at my church in 1985. Millard was an entrepreneur's entrepreneur. He built a successful business while attending law school and achieved financial independence at an early age. Together, Millard and his wife, Linda, decided that there is more to life than just making money, and they did something truly remarkable. They gave away all the money they had made and dedicated their lives to helping others. They took this action when they were young adults with four young children to raise.

They founded Habitat for Humanity in 1976 and the Fuller Center for Housing in 2005. Millard and Linda motivated millions of volunteers to share their wealth and talents to partner with their less fortunate neighbors to help them build their own homes. More than a million people live today in these houses, and the building continues. In 1996, Millard received the Presidential Medal of Freedom for "revolutionizing the way we look at charity." The Fuller Center for Housing continues the work that Millard and Linda started and has provided an opportunity for me, and many others who are fortunate enough to own their own homes, to help our hardworking low-income neighbors to build and own their homes.

Providing decent housing for the poor in a community dramatically improves that community. Well-housed students perform better in school. Well-housed employees are healthier, happier, and more productive at work. These new homeowners take a great deal of pride in their homes and take good care of them. They become involved in their community and take responsibility. They pay taxes and fight for issues that affect their community.

The Fuller Center for Housing is a nondenominational Christian organization that welcomes people of all faiths—or no faith at all—to join in eliminating the blight of poverty housing from our communities. In the richest nation in the world, it should be unacceptable for children to grow up in unhealthy, unsafe housing.

Volunteering for the Fuller Center has helped me to understand that each of us can change the world, one family at a time. Every home is a life-changing experience both for the families who live in the home and for the volunteers who help to build it.

Helping others can be a family adventure. All of my children have raised the money for and built a house for a family in need. Through the Fuller Center's Global Builders Program, you can combine an international family vacation with a volunteer experience that you will always remember. I encourage you to become involved. For current information on the Fuller Center for Housing and how you can get involved in eliminating poverty housing in your town, contact www.FullerCenter.org. I hope to see you on a build site one day soon.

Contact information for
The Fuller Center for Housing
P.O. Box 523
Americus, GA 31709
(229) 924-2900
www.fullercenter.org

Index

Index

Index

Index

Index

Index

Index

About the Author

John Schaub has successfully avoided holding a job since graduating from the University of Florida. He is an active investor who manages his own properties and investments. He shares what he has learned with other investors through his newsletter, recorded courses, and seminars.

John likes enjoying money as much as making it. He is an instrument-rated pilot and has piloted his own plane since 1973, and loves to sail, fish, ski, play tennis, and travel with his family.

He is an advocate for affordable housing and public education and has helped build more than 100 homes in the United States and other countries as chair of the Fuller Center for Housing and vice chair of Habitat for Humanity, International.

To Learn More from John

John teaches his well-known seminar twice a year. The class builds on the information in this book. Students learn the fine points of buying, financing, and managing property in today's market. As part of the class, students actually find and make offers to purchase houses at wholesale prices. For a schedule of John's courses, a copy of his newsletter, and a description of courses that John has recorded, go to **www.johnschaub .com**, or write to John Schaub at 2677 South Tamiami Trail, Suite 4, Sarasota, FL, 34239.